The Practical Guide to
Special Educational Needs in
Inclusive Primary Classrooms

The Practical Guide to Special Education Needs in Inclusive Primary Classrooms

Richard Rose and Marie Howley

Los Angeles | London | New Delhi
Singapore | Washington DC

First published 2007

Reprinted 2010

SAGE Publications Ltd
1 Oliver's Yard
55 City Road
London EC1Y 1SP

SAGE Publications Inc.
2455 Teller Road
Thousand Oaks, California 91320

SAGE Publications India Pvt Ltd
B 1/I 1 Mohan Cooperative Industrial Area
Mathura Road
New Delhi 110 044

SAGE Publications Asia-Pacific Pte Ltd
33 Pekin Street #02-01
Far East Square
Singapore 048763

Library of Congress control number 2006901468

A catalogue record for this book is available
from the British Library

ISBN 978-1-4129-2326-2
ISBN 978-1-4129-2327-9 (pbk)

Typeset by Pantek Arts Ltd, Maidstone, Kent
Printed in Great Britain by Ashford Colour Press Ltd, Gosport, Hampshire
Printed on paper from sustainable resources

Contents

Author notes

Richard Rose is Professor of Special and Inclusive Education at the Centre for Special Needs Education and Research, University of Northampton. He previously taught in schools in four English local authorities. Richard is co-author of several books dealing with special and inclusive schooling, including *Strategies to Promote Inclusive Practice* and *Encouraging Voices: Respecting the Insights of Young People Who Have Been Marginalised*.

Marie Howley is Senior Lecturer in Special Education at the Centre for Special Needs Education and Research, University of Northampton. Her research interests are largely in the area of pupils with autistic spectrum disorders. Marie's previous co-authored books include *Accessing the Curriculum for Pupils with Autistic Spectrum Disorders* and *Revealing the Hidden Code: Social Stories for People with Autistic Spectrum Disorders*.

Acknowledgements

This book would never have been written without the support of a number of important individuals. Liz Bonnett has provided first-class administrative support throughout. All of our colleagues in the Centre for Special Needs Education and Research (CeSNER) at the University of Northampton, and particularly Liz Waine, have informed our ideas and have been a source of great encouragement. Helen Fairlie at Sage has provided helpful advice throughout the writing and production process. Mayer-Johnson LLC*, and Widgit Software** gave us permission to use illustrations for which they have copyright. Finally, our families have, as ever, inspired and encouraged us. To all of these, we are indebted and say thank you.

*Mayer-Johnson LLC, PO Box 1579, Solana Beach, CA 92075, USA. Tel: 858 50 0084.
**Widgit Rebus Symbols © Widgit Software, www.Widgit.com. Tel: 01223 425558

Special educational needs (SEN) as a concept

Overview

This chapter will address the following issues:

- the development of special educational needs (SEN)as an issue for teachers
- provision for pupils with SEN
- the potential impact of labelling upon pupil self-perception
- teacher attitudes and expectations.

Introduction

In her seminal report of 1978, Mary Warnock (Department of Education and Science, 1978) suggested that as many as 20% of pupils have some form of SEN at some point in their school lives. If we accept her figure – and although it is one that we might dispute, it has been largely agreed by many authorities – it is evident that these pupils form a significant part of the overall school population and therefore require the careful attention of all teachers. Since the publication of the Warnock Report, advances in our understanding of pupils with SEN and the approaches to providing them with an appropriate education have been considerable. However, for many teachers, these pupils continue to provide a challenge and in some instances remain on the periphery of learning. The demands of learning present many pupils with difficulties that may damage their personal self-esteem to an extent that it deters them from making progress and in some instances leads to general disaffection with school. The demands of the curriculum, approaches to classroom management and organisation, the expectations of teachers and other adults, and the general ethos of the school are all factors which may support or impede the learning of pupils described as having SEN. These issues and the responsibility of class teachers to ensure their effective management form the basis of discussion in this book.

The term 'special educational needs' (SEN) was originally intended to provide an opportunity for schools, local education authorities and other service providers to ensure that pupils who have difficulties in learning or accessing the curriculum receive appropriate levels of support. The Education Act 1996 stated that:

> Children have special educational needs if they have a *learning difficulty*, which calls for special educational provision to be made for them

The Act went on to define a learning difficulty as being when children

a) have a significantly greater difficulty in learning than the majority of children of the same age; or

b) have a disability which prevents or hinders them from making use of educational facilities of a kind generally provided for children of the same age in schools within the area of the local education authority; or

c) are under compulsory school age and fall within the definition at (a) or (b) above or would do so if special educational provision was not made for them. (Education Act 1996, Section 312)

It is important to recognise that the definitions here provided establish a distinction between pupils with learning difficulties or disabilities who will require teachers to address their needs through modified teaching approaches or through specialist resources or curriculum modification, and others who, whilst possibly having a disability, may not require such modifications. Assumptions should not be made about the learning needs of pupils simply because they have a disability. Indeed, many pupils described as disabled perform well in schools and find that their disability has little or no impact upon their ability to access learning. Here, interpretation of the language within the definitions provided above is a critical factor. Applying labels to pupils, which may have deficit connotations or may be perceived in a negative manner could be a significant factor in lowering expectations and contributing to a failure in learning. Pupils with disabilities or clinical diagnoses have often been subjected to stereotyping that leads to discrimination in respect of the education with which they are provided. Many adults with disabilities have reflected upon their experiences of schooling and have had reason to recall with some resentment the low expectations of teachers, which inhibited their achievements and perpetuated negative images of them as individuals (Noble, 2003; Sainsbury, 2000; Souza, 1995, Toolan, 2003). When a label such as cerebral palsy or Asperger's syndrome is attached to pupils, it is often the case that even before meeting them teachers will have an image in their mind of the difficulties associated with teaching such individuals. Whilst it is undoubtedly true to say that an understanding of factors which might affect access to learning is of considerable help to the teacher, the low expectations which are often fuelled by disabling labels can lead to underachievement and a denial of entitlement to appropriate learning opportunities.

The term 'SEN' is one that has been subject to considerable debate in recent years. Bailey (1998) suggests that it is a difficult term because of its association with location. In many instances, pupils perceived as having SEN have received some or all of their teaching in an environment separate and different from that provided to their peers. Sometimes this has meant totally separate schooling in a special school or unit, and in other instances it may refer to the removal of pupils from classrooms for 'specialist' teaching or other interventions within a mainstream setting. Bailey (1998) asserts that pupils with special educational needs are often perceived as those who require access to a *service* that is different from that provided for other learners. Such a perception immediately informs teachers that they are likely to be required to provide intervention that is different from or additional to that provided for other pupils. Inevitably, this notion encourages the conscientious teacher to focus upon the needs of the individual and to attempt to devise ways of overcoming perceived barriers to learning. This focus upon individual needs may have both positive and negative outcomes. A recognition of individuality may encourage the teacher to examine pupil learning styles and preferences, and thereby enable an adjustment of teaching approaches to address these. Effective teachers differentiate their lessons to ensure that individual needs are recognised and planned for in a way that celebrates pupils' abilities rather than emphasising their difficulties. However, when teachers focus only upon what may be regarded as learning difficulties and adopt simplistic methods that aim to 'contain' pupils without due regard to their place within a group or whole class, they are as likely to damage the self-esteem of the individual as they are to encourage inclusion in learning.

Individuality is to be celebrated. Every learner is an individual, and the likelihood is that in most classes, all pupils will have strengths and weaknesses, preferences and dislikes, and interests and subjects which they find boring. The same is also true of teachers, as it is of everyone. Recognising individuality in learners is important, but must be managed in a way that puts neither the individual nor the class at a disadvantage. When teachers plan for an individual pupil, it is often the case that the work prepared is of equal value to others in the class. Singling out pupils for treatment that is different may simply draw attention to their difficulties and exacerbate the discrimination, which comes with a focus upon perceived deficiencies. The term 'SEN' can easily become pejorative. If it focuses upon the learning difficulties of the individual pupil, this may mean that pupils' strengths, personality, interests or abilities become secondary to the challenges that they face in learning. All teachers must ensure that they look beyond the simplistic use of labels to see pupils as individuals who, in common with all others, have needs (Norwich,

1996), and ensure that they are part of a community of learners sharing in the experiences of a whole class.

Teacher expectations are inevitably coloured by their previous experiences of teaching pupils. They are also subject to the influences of stereotyping and the mythologies and folklore of the staffroom. Pupils with SEN are generally regarded as presenting a challenge to the management and pedagogical skills of the teacher (Rose, 2001). It is certainly true to say that many pupils with SEN require particular interventions, in some instances, specialist resources or teaching approaches and additional attention to planning, in order to ensure that they receive effective access to learning. However, the overgeneralisation of pupil needs on the basis of a special needs label is not helpful to teachers attempting to provide effective learning opportunities. For example, whilst you may have had experience of teaching a pupil with a recognised diagnosis, such as autistic spectrum disorder (ASD) or attention-deficit and hyperactivity disorder (ADHD), this is not an indication that the next pupil encountered with such a label will learn, behave or react in the same way as the first such individual. In addition, there are established teaching approaches that have proven effective with some pupils who have received specific diagnoses. For example, 'structured teaching' (Schopler et al., 1995) and 'social stories' (Gray, 1998) are two methods often cited as efficacious in the education of pupils with ASD. It would be erroneous to suggest that these approaches, having worked with some pupils with ASD, will therefore be effective with all pupils who have been subject to this diagnosis. Similarly, it is a narrow interpretation of teaching to suggest that these teaching methods, having been developed for use with pupils with ASD, may not have benefits for other learners who do not have this label. You will need to develop an approach to teaching that is receptive to new ideas and techniques. However, you will also need to consider these in a more critical manner that looks beyond the narrow application for which they have often been designed. Teaching systems developed to address a specific population may be transferable for use with other learners, but teachers looking for a ready-made, off-the-shelf system that will meet the challenges of teaching are likely to be disappointed.

As a teacher who is new to the profession, whilst needing to be aware of the many benefits of learning from more experienced colleagues, you will also need to be wary of the teacher who is quick to forecast difficulties. Warnings of family traits – *this pupil will give you grief, I taught his elder brother and the whole family is nothing but trouble* – or stereotypic views of individuals – *all pupils with Down's syndrome are stubborn and difficult in class*, are both discriminatory and unfounded. All pupils, regardless of need and ability, exhibit personal learning traits and behaviours, that single them out as individuals. Whilst much is known about the likely challenges faced by pupils with specific diagnoses such as ASD or Down's syndrome, each will be characterised by individuality as a learner. Predictions based upon stereotypes are responsible for the self-fulfilling prophecies that result in low expectations, and underachievement. As you develop your skills as a professional, you must gain the confidence to make your own assessments of the learning needs of individuals, and to avoid being influenced by those who perceive pupils as 'types' rather than individual learners.

Changing patterns of need and provision

The majority of pupils with SEN are educated in mainstream schools. This has always been the situation, and whilst a small percentage of the overall population of pupils with SEN receive their education in segregated special provision, teachers have always accepted that they will have pupils in their class who present difficulties with learning. However, it is possible to observe some changes in the population of mainstream classrooms, as a result of both societal changes and the implementation of legislation. These changes mean that teachers are at times likely to encounter pupils with more complex needs in their classrooms than might have been the case 15 or 20 years ago. These influences upon change are likely to persist and are therefore worthy of some further consideration.

Advances in obstetric practice mean that many children who in previous years would have had little chance of surviving to school age are now entering schools. Whilst this improvement in life chances for these pupils should be welcomed, a significant number of such children are likely to exhibit a range of learning needs. At the same time, there appears to be a significant increase in the incident of specific disorders, such as ASD and ADHD, in many schools. This change in demographics is beyond the control of teachers and therefore should concern you only in respect of ensuring that you develop a range of teaching strategies suitable to meet the complex needs of a diverse school population. The promotion of a more inclusive education system must be welcomed for the opportunities that are being afforded to pupils who in previous years might have been denied effective teaching or the chance to interact with their peers. There is now an increased imperative for all teachers to ensure that they develop their professional skills, knowledge and understanding in a way that enhances the learning opportunities for all pupils.

In recent years, the training of teachers has become a largely technocratic process more concerned with a focus upon procedure and providing fundamental professional skills than on encouraging new teachers to reflect upon processes of teaching and learning (Garner, 2001). Teaching is a challenging profession and requires that you develop a wide range of skills in managing your classroom. However, in order to develop optimum effectiveness, you need to acquire the ability to interrogate your own practice, analyse its effectiveness, in relation to a wide range of pupil needs, and adjust your teaching in order to address these. Such a professional approach should be founded upon a recognition that learning to be an effective teacher is a challenging mission which requires continuous updating of knowledge and a willingness to apply this new learning to a wide range of teaching situations. In addition, it demands that you challenge your own thinking about how individual pupils learn and recognise that your responsibility to address the needs of all pupils in a class is most readily addressed through an analysis of pupil needs within a whole-class context. The demands of the curriculum and an inordinate concentration upon attainment against national expectations, whilst not always acknowledging other learning outcomes, can sometimes appear to militate against the conscientious teacher (Booth, Ainscow and Dyson, 1997). The most effective teachers rise to this challenge and are able to ensure that the individuality of learners is addressed whilst maintaining an overview of whole classes of pupils. In some schools, pupils who have been labelled as having SEN are regarded as a threat to the ability of teachers to maintain high academic standards and achieve the desired learning outcomes. However, the most effective teachers often find that by planning to address the needs of these pupils they devise approaches which are not only successful for the targeted individual, but also have a positive impact upon other learners in the class.

Emerging ideas of service delivery

Whilst inclusion has quite rightly led to a reappraisal of the ways in which mainstream primary schools address the education of pupils described as having SEN, most local authorities continue to maintain some specialist provision. Special schools have long played a major role in addressing the needs of those pupils deemed to have the most complex learning needs (Mittler, 2000). However, it is now largely accepted that pupils should be assigned a special school placement only when it is clear that mainstream schools are unable to meet their learning needs. Recent legislation and advisory documentation (DfEE, 1997, DfES, 2003a; OfSTED, 2004) has called for greater collaboration between mainstream and special schools. In some instances, this has led to formal partnerships being established between mainstream and special schools. Often, such partnerships have been designed either to aid the transition of pupils from special into mainstream schools (Rose and Coles, 2002), or to ensure that teachers benefit from the expertise of teachers who have an established commitment to working with pupils with SEN (McLeod, 2001). However, teachers in mainstream schools may also be able to learn from some of the approaches to teaching or about the creation of learning environments more commonly associated with teaching in a special school. Pupils with SEN have at times led teachers to reconsider their teaching strategies. This in turn has encouraged the introduction of specific approaches that have enabled curriculum access where previously pupils have been unable to participate effectively in learning. Examples of this include the introduction of structured teaching, as advocated by the Treatment and Education for Autistic and

Related Communication Handicapped Children (TEACCH) programme, which has supported teachers of pupils with ASD in gaining curriculum access (Mesibov and Howley, 2003), or the use of symbols or other approaches to augmentative communication, which has allowed pupils with communication difficulties to participate (Latham and Miles, 2001).

As a teacher working in a primary school, you should become familiar with some of the approaches that have become common practice in special provision. Often, teachers working in special schools or units have had to adjust their practices and devise strategies to ensure access to learning or increased participation. It is certainly true that many of these strategies will not easily transfer to a mainstream classroom without modification. It is equally clear that, where teachers have been prepared to make adaptations, either to their own teaching, or to the classroom environment, this has had benefits for learners who have otherwise struggled. As mainstream and special schools begin to work more closely together, opportunities for sharing ideas about effective teaching and learning are likely to emerge. The movement of practices between phases of school provision is likely to prove beneficial, but only where innovative teachers demonstrate a willingness to engage in debate about the implementation and efficacy of new ideas, and to make changes in their own practice. For many teachers, such a challenge will be welcomed as they maintain a focus upon the needs of all learners in their classrooms. For others, the demands made by pupils with SEN and the suggestion that changes in practice may be necessary could be regarded as threatening. Communication between teachers and the provision of effective support networks which encourage reflective classroom enquiry and enable a sharing of ideas are essential if the needs of a complex school population are to be addressed.

An emerging model of schooling in which partnership between mainstream and special provision plays a key role will not only depend upon the policy decisions of local authorities, but will also require the enthusiasm of individual teachers, such as you, who are prepared to assess continually their own skills and understanding. Recent moves toward establishing a more interdisciplinary approach to the management of children under the *Every Child Matters* (2003) agenda should provide increased opportunities for developing effective support networks for all children. It should also encourage teachers to play a leading role in enabling a change in current concepts of special educational needs. To date, this concept has tended to focus upon perceived pupil learning deficits and has encouraged a belief that pupils labelled as 'special' are in some way making additional demands upon schools. The agenda of *Every Child Matters* requires that all agencies that are concerned for the welfare of children, including schools, refocus their attention to ensure that needs are addressed under the following five imperatives:

- Be healthy.
- Stay safe.

- Enjoy and achieve.
- Make a positive contribution.
- Achieve economic well-being.

These five headings apply to all pupils and do not distinguish whether individuals are labelled as able, or have learning difficulties or disability. Schools must consider how they provide a learning environment and create an ethos, that encourages each of these five factors. The emphasis here is as much about pupil well-being as it is about academic outcomes or attainment of preordained targets. This is not to suggest that these indicators will not remain important. Indeed, it may justifiably be argued that making a positive contribution to society and achieving economic well-being is most readily achieved when pupils have attained a higher level of academic knowledge and understanding. However, a commitment to focusing upon 'the whole child', as required under this critical legislation, should enable teachers and schools to develop policies and practices that increasingly celebrate the diversity of needs and abilities within a school population. Lumsden (2005) has highlighted many of the challenges which inter-agency working will bring to professionals who are committed to enhancing the opportunities of learners. She emphasises the need for all concerned to develop an understanding of professional roles based upon respect and reciprocity, and suggests that this will be achieved only when effective lines of communication between you as a teacher and the other key players in your pupils' lives are opened and maintained. Your attitude to other non-teaching professional colleagues will greatly influence the effectiveness of the support provided to pupils.

These are exciting times to be a teacher in our schools. However, we are also in an era where expectations and demands change quickly, and teachers are required to respond appropriately and in the best interest of all pupils. Concepts that have been long established, such as SEN, are being increasingly challenged, as our understanding increases and our expectation rises. This change should be welcomed, particularly where it influences practice for improvements in the lives of pupils. However, as with all change, a successful outcome for pupils will depend upon a teaching profession that maintains a positive outlook for all pupils and is prepared to be innovative and committed to a search for the most effective means of ensuring that all pupils learn.

Questions and issues for reflection

- To what extent does the labelling of pupils as having SEN affect my expectations of their performance?
- How aware am I of specialist teaching approaches that may enable pupils in my class to achieve greater access to learning?
- What are the factors which currently influence the ways in which I view the learning potential of my pupils?

Conclusion

All teachers, regardless of their experience and expertise face daily challenges from pupils who appear not to respond to their usual teaching approaches. One of the most interesting aspects of being a teacher is that new challenges appear all the time, and that this requires tenacity and professionalism in order to be successful. As a new teacher you will soon realise the need to review continually your own work, and that the benefits of gaining new understanding and knowledge are a critical aspect of your professionalism. On too many occasions in the past, pupils described as having SEN have been regarded as being a problem. Sadly, you will often hear your professional peers referring to some of the pupils in their classes in negative terms. The act of teaching cannot be divorced from human rights issues and must begin with a commitment on your part to respect all of the pupils in your class and try to see the world from their set of experiences. This is a difficult thing to ask of any teacher, but the efforts which you make to understand the lives of the pupils in your class will provide benefits in terms of your appreciation of the challenges which they face and may enable you to further your empathy with those who experience difficulties with learning. Such pupils are less of a source of difficulty than is our inability to understand how we can develop our own teaching skills and understanding in order to include them effectively in our classrooms. The teaching profession is blessed with having many thousands of committed professionals who continue to strive to learn and understand more about how we can improve the lives and enhance the learning opportunities for all pupils. Your commitment to this cause can add significantly to our knowledge of how better to address the needs of pupils who have often found themselves marginalised within our schools.

2 Becoming an inclusive teacher

Overview

This chapter will address the following issues:

- defining educational inclusion
- teacher influences upon inclusive learning
- individual pupil needs within whole-class contexts.

Introduction

The term 'inclusion' has been generally accepted as common parlance within today's education system and indeed in wider society. The inequalities of the past often led to the exclusion and isolation of individuals who were perceived as different and sometimes inferior by dint of their needs, abilities, social class, race, gender or culture. As a commitment to the endorsement of policies which promote equality has been achieved, so has it been recognised as wholly inappropriate to provide a school curriculum that provides, for example, experiences to boys from which girls are excluded, or the teaching of literature or music based solely upon a monocultural interpretation. Such were the practices of the past, and it has taken many years to begin to break down those barriers, which denied so many pupils an opportunity to fulfil their true potential. This is not to suggest that the struggle to provide a more equitable education system has been fully won. Indeed, it would be naive in the extreme to suggest that prejudicial attitudes to individuals and groups do not persist to some extent even today in our schools (Barton, 2003; Helavaara Robertson and Hill, 2001). Marginalisation continues to sour the educational experiences of a significant number of pupils within our society, and teachers must accept the challenge of addressing this issue in order to promote a more equitable education system. The majority of teachers demonstrate a daily commitment to ensuring the well-being and improving the educational opportunities of all pupils in their class. This does not detract from the need to be vigilant in ensuring that teaching approaches and attitudes in the classroom demand that the needs of all pupils are recognised and appropriate steps taken to enable every pupil to learn.

The whole tenor of inclusive education has been founded upon a recognition that much remains to be achieved in providing schools which meet the needs of all pupils regardless of need, ability or cultural heritage. The attention given to this issue in recent years has been extensive, but would not have been so had there not been a clear recognition of the denial of opportunities for learning experienced by some sections of our population. Inclusion has become a topical issue, but one that continues to bring challenges to teachers and policy makers alike. Our understanding of an education system that fully addresses the needs of all pupils has developed considerably over the past 20 years, but remains far from complete. This is not to deny the commitment which teachers and others in schools have given to this complex matter, but it more likely reflects the difficulties of fully understanding the ways in which we can create learning environments that are truly inclusive for all learners. In this chapter, we will examine the challenges which teachers are attempting to address on a daily basis, and will consider what is known about promoting more inclusive practice through a review of teaching. This can be achieved only if we consider the definition and nature of inclusion early in a discussion of the critical aspects of pedagogy, classroom management and attitudinal influences that can support or deny greater access to learning.

Seeking a definition of inclusion

Florian (1998) has identified a significant number of definitions of inclusion from both the UK and further afield. Each of these definitions has in common a commitment to enabling pupils who have been marginalised, including those with special educational needs (SEN), to receive improved social and learning opportunities alongside their peers. In particular, the notion of pupils with SEN being provided with the opportunity to be educated alongside those who are not labelled in this way is seen as a priority. However, Florian acknowledges an important factor here in recognising that, for many teachers, pupils with significant SEN will continue to pose a challenge requiring careful planning and in some cases the adoption of teaching approaches specifically aimed at meeting individual needs. Inclusion is not simply about placing pupils with SEN in mainstream classrooms. Once located within this environment, pupils must be afforded opportunities to learn at an appropriate pace and level and be enabled to socialise with their peers whilst taking their place as equal members of the school community. In some instances, this will demand the use of strategies and approaches which are directly aimed at encouraging positive interaction and fostering learning for all pupils. It is simplistic in the extreme to believe that pupils will learn simply because they are placed in a mainstream classroom. Teachers have a duty to consider how each pupil will access learning, and to identify how individual learning needs and preferred learning styles can best be addressed. It is now largely recognised that teachers who are able to adapt their teaching approaches in order to address the learning difficulties of one pupil, often benefit others in the class (Ainscow, 1999) and that flexibility is a critical feature of inclusive classrooms.

Some teachers and parents express an understandable anxiety that pupils with SEN may detract from the learning of others in the classroom. In particular, those pupils who exhibit difficult behaviours may be seen as making inordinate demands upon teacher time. Teachers do need to be aware that when planning lessons particular attention will need to be given to ensuring that the work provided is at an appropriate level to meet the needs of all pupils. Disruptive behaviours often occur as a result of lessons that place either too much or too little demand upon pupils. Lessons that are interesting, stimulating and differentiated to meet a range of needs and abilities are less likely to be subject to disruption. Similarly, the careful organisation of classroom groups and the provision of appropriate resources and levels of support will have a direct impact upon the ability of pupils with SEN to participate fully in lessons.

Even the best organised and most effective teachers occasionally have difficulties in managing some pupils with SEN. Indeed, there are a few pupils whose behaviour or learning difficulties are so complex that even with support they appear difficult to maintain in a mainstream classroom. It is not our contention that in today's educational climate every school will be able to educate successfully every pupil. Currently, there remains a need for highly specialist provision for some pupils that will most likely be found in a special school or unit. Despite the need for specialist provision for some, many pupils with SEN are now educated in inclusive mainstream settings. Class teachers have a clear responsibility to all pupils in their class to explore different teaching approaches and strategies and to manage their classrooms in ways that encourage pupil participation and full access to learning. There will be times when all teachers need to call upon the additional expertise that exists in school, possibly from the SEN coordinator (SENCO), or to seek assistance from outside agencies that can offer specific advice. When this is necessary, teachers should not regard this as a display of weakness or failure to perform at a required level, but should rather consider it a necessary part of working to support a pupil within a multidisciplinary regime. Indeed, the *Every Child Matters* agenda, which has encouraged the development of greater integration within services to children, is already influencing moves toward greater coordination of multidisciplinary responses to the needs of individuals. All teachers can do much to promote the inclusion of pupils with SEN, and the majority will succeed most of the time. It is important that all teachers learn from their experiences of working with such pupils and demonstrate an ability to adjust their teaching practices and seek solutions to the learning difficulties experienced by some pupils.

Key questions and issues for reflection:

- How does my school define inclusion?
- How do school policies influence expectations of pupils with SEN?

Inclusive teaching

All effective teaching begins from a positive attitude and a desire to achieve what is best for all the pupils in a class. Barnes (1999) has emphasised the impact of positive thinking and attitudes upon the management of successful classrooms. He suggests that, when confronted by challenges in the classroom, teachers need to develop powers of objectivity to enable them to recognise the difficulties that they face and take logical steps to addressing them. Some teachers enter the classroom with less than positive attitudes toward individual pupils. If pupils have been given a label, such as behavioural difficulty or ADHD, this can increase teacher anxiety and lead to a lowering of expectation. It is essential that we remember that such labels are no more than broad descriptors. There are no 'typical' pupils with ADHD, Down's syndrome or any other condition, and therefore our expectations should be governed by the actual performance and needs of the individual pupil rather than by some mythological generalisation of need based upon a somewhat dubious system of labelling. Positive teachers expect all of their pupils to learn, and they try to enable them to reach their optimum levels of performance. This, of course, does not imply that all pupils will learn at the same pace or that they will have similar aptitudes, interests or needs. However, as a starting point, teachers must recognise that their primary responsibility is to address the needs of all pupils in the class, including those who offer the greatest resistance to learning. Jupp (1992) suggests that teachers need to develop a child-centred personal philosophy that begins with the belief that all pupils can learn and that the skill of effective teachers can enable any pupil to do so. This is certainly a philosophy that we endorse. Other researchers (Ellins and Porter, 2005; Wilkins and Nietfield, 2004) have similarly demonstrated how different teacher attitudes can affect the learning outcomes of individual pupils described as having SEN. It is up to all teachers to begin with an expectation that pupils will learn rather than to make assumptions that they will fail.

In recent years, there has been a debate about whether there is a specific form of pedagogy that is most appropriate for pupils with SEN (Kershner and Florian, 2004; Lewis, 2000; Lewis and Norwich, 2001). Most of the researchers engaged in this debate suggest that, whilst there are certainly teaching approaches which have been developed by teachers of pupils with SEN, these are likely to benefit all learners and are not only of specific value to selected groups of pupils. Many teachers who have considerable experience of working with pupils with complex needs, including those working in special schools, have devised approaches and adopted techniques to promote greater access to learning or have attempted to overcome specific barriers for some pupils. Examples of this may include the use of an augmentative system of communication, such as Makaton (a form of sign language) or a symbol system to support pupils who have difficulties with language. Similarly, the use of structured teaching, which has found favour with many teachers of pupils with autistic spectrum disorder (ASD), or kinaesthetic approaches for learners with dyslexia have often proved successful for specific groups of learners. However, in a review of teaching strategies and approaches for pupils with SEN, Davis and Florian (2004) concluded that whilst many strategies and approaches are being adopted for teaching pupils with SEN, there has been insufficient investigation into their efficacy in order to reach definitive conclusions about many of these. This conclusion suggests that teachers should give greater consideration to assessing the impact of the strategies that they develop to address the needs of pupils who challenge their conventional methods.

All teachers should consider two important points when contemplating the methods that they may adopt in working with pupils with SEN. Firstly, there is little evidence to support a belief that one model of teaching will address the needs of all pupils. Joyce, Calhoun and Hopkins (2002) have demonstrated how different learning situations and individual learners benefit from a range of teaching approaches. Whilst some learners, including those with SEN, will feel most comfortable when working within one model, learning becomes most effective when they can adapt to a range of different models. Similarly, the teacher who feels at home with one approach to teaching and sticks to this is unlikely to be addressing the needs of all learners in the class. Effective teachers learn to adjust their teaching to address particular teaching situations and the needs of their classes.

A second point relates to the nature of many of the specialist approaches that are seen in use with pupils with SEN. Many of these are used to provide effective access for learners. The use of augmentative communication as described above would be one particular example of this. For pupils with speech and language difficulties, the use of signs and symbols to augment the spoken word may afford them opportunities to participate in class which would otherwise have not existed. The use of technological aids, such as computer access switches or adapted keyboards for pupils with physical difficulties or sensory impairments, is another example of providing access to enable participation. These particular actions may not in themselves constitute a means of promoting learning, but, as Kershner (2000) points out, without the provision of effective access, opportunities for learning may well be denied.

When considering the implementation of a specialist teaching approach, you need to ask a series of questions which will ensure that the management and effectiveness of the approach can be secured.

What do I anticipate the pupil will gain from this approach?

You need to feel confident that the approach to be adopted will genuinely afford the pupil better opportunities for learning. When feeling concerned that a pupil is making insufficient progress, teachers will sometimes grasp at straws and reach for any resource or approach that seems to provide an alternative. This can at times lead to frustration when a newly adopted approach fails to yield results or benefits. It is important that teachers consider carefully why they are choosing to use an approach and identify intended learning outcomes for the pupil. If possible, it is advisable to discuss specific approaches with teachers who have used them before. The SENCO can be a critical point of contact here, should be able to provide advice and may even help with monitoring. Consider also how long it may take before any effects of an approach may be seen. When a new technique or method is adopted, it will take time for the teacher to gain confidence in its use and for the pupil to adapt to materials. When pupils are having difficulties with learning, they need time to adjust to new ideas and will need extra support and coaching until they gain confidence.

How manageable will this be in the general teaching situation?

You will need to manage whole classes, and whilst the introduction of innovative methods or materials may have major benefits for an individual, it is important to consider the impact upon the whole class. Often teachers find that materials or approaches that they introduce for one pupil have benefits for others in the class. It may be worth considering the adoption of an approach for several class members who will then be able to share in activities and discussion of their work. It is important to estimate how much additional time will be needed to support individual pupils who are using a resource that is different from that available to their peers. It may be possible in some cases to allocate a teaching assistant (TA) to work with a pupil in this situation. However, if part of the intended outcomes of learning for the pupil is to gain in independence and confidence, the teacher will need to ensure that dependency is not being created through allocation of a TA to an individual pupil for an excessive amount of time. The teacher will also need to consider factors associated with distraction. To what extent does the resource provided for one pupil detract from the learning of others? Such a factor might determine where the pupil is located in the class and when specific resources are used.

How will I transfer this approach to other teaching and learning situations?

Consistency and application of learning are important factors in determining the success of pupils. If an approach is introduced in one subject in order to provide access to or support for learning, the teacher must ensure that this is generalised throughout the teaching process. For example, if a pupil with learning difficulties has difficulties with reading and writing and a decision is made to introduce an augmentative communication system, such as the use of symbols, as a primary mode of communication, this must be consistently applied. Making use of symbols only in English lessons and then depending upon traditional orthography in, for example, geography would not be of great benefit to the pupil. When considering the introduction of any specialist approach, teachers must review the whole teaching process across the timetable in order to be sure of the implications of such a move. This also, of course, means involving other staff who may come into contact with the pupil at different times of the week. Pupils who receive specialist support through equipment often report their frustration when a successful approach is available only at limited times or when supported by specific members of staff.

Who else needs to be aware of what I am doing, and what is the implication for them?

Everyone who comes into contact with a pupil needs to know if particular approaches or resources are being used. Unless individuals are familiar with the requirements to use specific approaches, they cannot be expected to support the teaching and learning of the pupil. In some instances, this will mean communicating beyond the teaching staff to involve other colleagues, such as lunchtime supervisors, who may come into contact with a pupil. For example, pupils who are provided with a visual timetable to assist them in knowing what to do at specific times may become frustrated if adults are not aware of this and do not allow the pupil enough time to consult this important supportive material.

Contact with parents is clearly important when considering innovation with an individual pupil. If parents feel that their son or daughter is being treated differently without an adequate explanation of why decisions have been made, they may disapprove and feel that the school is not keeping them informed. Most parents welcome the introduction of specific approaches which are designed to help with access and learning, but it is essential for teachers to ensure that a clear explanation and justification of methods is provided.

Are there resource implications in using this approach?

The introduction of any new teaching approach is likely to have resource implications. If you give a commitment to using a new approach, such as the introduction of 'social stories' for a pupil with ASD, or the use of an overlay board to access a computer, this is likely to make demands upon time both within the classroom and in preparing materials. Pupils and teachers will become frustrated if a system is introduced and then fails because it is not adequately resourced. The introduction of a teaching approach that falters because of the lack of availability of necessary materials will damage the confidence of all involved in the learning process. You must be organised and plan ahead either for the production of more materials or the introduction of supportive approaches.

How will the approach be introduced to the pupil?

Pupils who are aware of their own difficulties with learning need to feel confident that new ideas introduced by the teacher are designed to be supportive and are well focused on individual needs. Awareness of intended outcomes is essential. You need to communicate clearly to the pupil why an approach has been introduced and how support will be provided. The pupil needs to be confident that this is an intervention which will make life easier and have definite learning benefits. It is necessary to spend time explaining how an approach is intended to work and what the pupil can do to assist in this process. It is equally important to protect the pupil's self esteem. If individual pupils feel that they are being singled out for treatment different from that afforded to their peers, they may feel self-conscious or embarrassed. Often it is best to involve other pupils in the introduction of new approaches and to ensure that the pupil does not become isolated as the only person using a piece of equipment or other materials. Some pupils will enjoy being singled out by a piece of equipment or approach. For example, a pupil who requires an adapted keyboard in order to access a computer because of a physical disability may well like to demonstrate its use to others in the class and could well be perceived by other pupils as having specific skills that they do not have.

Before introducing any innovation, the teacher should discuss it with the pupil, who will be able to advise the teacher on how to approach this situation. Pupils are very conscious of the efforts of teachers to provide additional support and will value being consulted at the earliest stages. Similarly, any TA or other adult who is to be involved in this process needs to be engaged in discussion at an early stage in order to ensure confidence in the materials and the requirements of the teacher.

Are there professional development implications?

Some specialised teaching approaches can be introduced into classrooms with minimal requirements for training. However, some, such as the use of signed communication or the introduction of an electronic communication device, will require the development of new skills and understanding. For example, the introduction into a class of a deaf pupil who is dependent upon British Sign Language would require the support of a skilled signed communicator in order to ensure that the pupil gains full benefit and access. Whilst, in this case, the teacher may not become a fully qualified signer, a basic understanding which enables social interaction with the pupil is desirable. When considering the introduction of an approach or new teaching materials, teachers should spend time prior to their introduction familiarising themselves with the materials and their workings. Pupils will lose patience and confidence if teachers appear to lack an understanding of what they are doing. For example, the teacher who introduces a software package to help a pupil overcome a maths problem and then spends half of a lesson trying to read a manual or sort out an access difficulty will quickly lose the confidence of the pupil. Sometimes it may be effective to examine new materials with the pupil and to discuss how these will be introduced and used.

Do I see this as a long-term measure or one from which I hope eventually to move the pupil forward to the approaches commonly used in the class?

Some specialist teaching materials may be introduced to overcome specific problems with the anticipation that they are only a short-term measure. If this is the case, you must consider how to make the transition to the approaches in common use in the class. Short-term measures must be used in a way that does not create dependency. You should produce an exit strategy which identifies when the specialist approach or materials will have served their purpose and how to reintroduce the pupil to the generally used methods.

For some pupils, strategies and approaches will be long term, and through these, pupils will be included in learning which would otherwise be denied. This may well be the case with augmentative forms of communication or the use of technology. Where such long-term implications exist, you must ensure the careful transition from one class to another and in some instances from the primary to the secondary school. This will require careful communication with receiving colleagues well in advance of the pupil's move. Time must be allowed for teachers and other colleagues receiving pupils to have training, and there may be a need to plan for the transfer or acquisition of essential resources. Pupils need to feel confident that interventions upon which they have become dependent and through which they have benefited will continue to be there as a critical form of support.

Inclusive teaching requires that teachers ensure that all pupils in a class are able to access learning. This means not only planning to address individual needs, but doing this in the context of a whole-class situation and with due regard to the impact of any actions upon all learners. The term 'differentiation' has become familiar to most colleagues working in today's classrooms. Planning to address a wide range of needs within a single class requires that teachers be able to provide work at different levels, deliver this at a variable pace and use a diversity of resources according to the needs of individuals (O'Brien and Guiney, 2001). Whilst differentiation is clearly important and can enable teachers to be confident that they are addressing the needs of a wide range of learners, there is a need to exercise some caution with regard to its management and delivery. Good practice in differentiating teaching and learning requires a detailed understanding of the needs of all pupils in the class. Simply giving a pupil with SEN work that is less demanding than that given to others is not adequate. The work needs to be tailored to the individual needs, preferred learning style and current level of learning of the pupil. It also needs to provide sufficient challenge to enable pupils to progress and not remain static in their current learning. At times, what passes for differentiation is no better than discrimination. If all that is achieved is the presentation of work to pupils, that keeps them occupied but does not advance their learning, we are not providing an adequate service to the individual. Learning occurs when pupils can do something or know information that they could not do or did not know before the teaching process was undertaken. All pupils must be challenged to learn regardless of need or ability.

Lewis (1992) identified 12 forms of differentiation which teachers may use in order to support learning:

Differentiation of content: e.g. pupils in a group all work toward a single aim, such as reading competence, but use several different reading schemes to get there.

Differentiation by interest: e.g. all pupils are producing graphs, but their graphs represent different data according to personal interest.

Differentiation of pace: all pupils work at the same task, or with the same materials, but the teacher has different expectations of the time required for completion.

Differentiation of access: materials or methods of working are different for individual pupils. E.g. whilst one pupil writes with a pencil, another uses a computer and another produces pictorial work.

Differentiation of outcome: e.g. one pupil writes a story, another draws a picture to tell the story and another records the story on audio tape.

Differentiation of curricular sequence: pupils enter the curriculum at different points or take part in the curriculum in a different order from that of their peers.

Differentiation of structure: some pupils work on step by step (task analysed curriculum) whilst others work on 'chunks'.

Differentiation of teacher time: the teacher gives more time to some pupils during specific tasks in order to ensure access.

Differentiation of teaching style: e.g. some pupils may require individual instruction whilst others can work in small groups or pairs.

Differentiation of level: all pupils work through a similar sequence, in maths for example, but at a variety of levels.

Differentiation by grouping: the teacher groups particular pupils together for specific activities. Pupils act as supporters, or work with peers with whom they are comfortable or confident. (Lewis, 1992, pp24–5)

Each of these approaches can prove useful in the armoury of the teacher, and you should expect to consider these in respect of both the individual pupil and the context in which teaching is taking place. When planning to address individual needs, teachers should contemplate how their actions will be viewed by all pupils in the class. High expectations of all pupils are essential. When presenting work to pupils that is different from that provided for their peers, it is necessary to ensure that this is not seen as a soft option or a form of favouritism. Whenever possible, it is advisable to give several pupils the same work in order that they can discuss this, share ideas and feel that they are part of the group. Work differentiated for one pupil will often benefit others in the class. By bringing pupils together to work, it is possible to encourage peer support and even peer coaching, benefiting both pupils with SEN and the more able pupils who need to think through ideas as they provide support. In an inclusive classroom, all pupils feel that they have a part to play, and differentiation is viewed as a way of ensuring that everyone participates. Where work is prepared solely for an individual pupil, if this is not effectively managed, it may result in isolation or feelings of resentment.

Andy is a teacher in a Year 6 class in a primary school. In his class, he has two pupils who have SEN. Sharon is a wheelchair-user who has cerebral palsy. She has limited use of her hands and poor control of her limbs. However, Sharon is one of the most academically able pupils in the class and is a very responsive learner. Callum has general learning difficulties and finds it hard to concentrate for more than a few minutes. He is often apprehensive about the introduction of new ideas and is very conscious that he finds learning more challenging than his peers.

In an English lesson today, Andy is working with his class on writing a report of a visit which they recently made to a local museum to visit the collection of Egyptian artefacts. During the visit, each member of the class was asked to choose an object to research and to produce a picture of the selected item to take back to school. Most of the class were provided with coloured pencils and paper to produce their pictures. However, Sharon has difficulty controlling a pencil, so Andy provided her and two of her classmates with a digital camera to take some pictures. Sharon's lack of control meant that taking pictures with the camera required the use of a tripod to obtain a steady image. Her two friends assisted her in positioning and stabilising the tripod, whilst Sharon selected an Egyptian statue of the god Horus to photograph from different angles. Callum enjoys drawing and has no difficulty with completing a picture. However, in order to make notes about this, Andy allows him to dictate his ideas and the findings from his research to Mandy, a parent who has joined them on the trip.

In the English lesson, the pupils are writing their accounts. Sharon uses a computer with an adapted keyboard which has large keys and a guard to prevent her hitting the wrong keys when writing her report. This is a slow process and Andy is careful to tell her how much he expects her to write. He pairs her with the two classmates who worked with her at the museum, and the three pupils negotiate what they are going to write so that at the end of the lesson they can combine their work.

Callum is paired with a more able pupil, Mark. He has the notes from the visit which he dictated to Mandy. The two pupils discuss what Callum had found out, and they work together to write their report. Callum's partner does most of the writing, but Andy insists that Callum also writes his section. This is achieved by making a game in which Mark writes sentences, leaving out a word from each sentence. Mark reads each sentence to Callum, who has to guess the missing word and then write it in.

In the preceeding case study, the teacher has demonstrated an awareness of the challenges which the pupils with SEN in his class face in accessing learning. He has planned effectively to differentiate activities for the needs of both pupils in a way which ensures that learning is a social activity and fully includes the individuals within their class. In the terms set out by Lewis, above, Andy has used differentiation by *access, outcome, structure* and *grouping* in order to ensure that Sharon and Callum are fully included in the lessons. Andy has also encouraged and made effective use of peer support to ensure that these two pupils feel that they are fully engaged with their classmates.

Key questions and issues for reflection

- How does planning to meet the needs of one pupil affect the learning of others?
- What processes are in place to assess the effectiveness and potential impact of specialist teaching approaches?
- How are professional development needs identified before implementing specialist approaches or using specialist resources?
- How can best use be made of the SENCO in securing advice about addressing individual needs?
- How many forms of differentiation are being regularly deployed in the class and how are judgements made about which approaches to use?

Conclusion

Becoming an inclusive primary schoolteacher is dependent first of all upon a belief not only that all pupils have an entitlement to learn, but also that they are capable of so doing. However, attitude and belief alone are insufficient to enable the teacher to become effective. Teachers need to ensure that their commitment to inclusion is supported by an understanding of how pupils learn and enhanced by an appreciation of the approaches and resources which are proving effective with a diverse pupil population. There are many resources, schemes and systems available commercially which claim to have benefits for pupils with special educational needs. Some of these are well substantiated through many years of successful use by teachers. Others require greater caution and should be examined in detail before committing to them. The advice of the SENCO and more experienced teachers, or of those working for support services, may be crucial in making the right decisions. However, in the early stages of teaching, all teachers have a preferred approach to teaching and need to identify those resources with which they personally feel comfortable. As teachers gain in confidence, they should ensure that they expand their personal teaching styles and become responsive to teaching in a variety of ways which suit changing circumstances. Teachers who adhere to a narrow set of teaching approaches are unlikely to thrive in an inclusive primary school. Effective teachers are responsive but not reactive. They contemplate the challenges faced by pupils, try to analyse these in respect of both their own experience and the perspective of the pupil, and plan actions on the basis of this analysis. Becoming skilled in this way takes time, and all teachers, even the most experienced, need to seek the advice of others when confronting new challenges. Schools will be inclusive only at the point when teachers feel that they are equipped to meet the needs of all pupils in their classes. This will inevitably take time, but it must begin with a commitment on the part of individual teachers to gain the necessary skills and understanding to support a diverse range of pupil needs.

3 Pupils giving cause for concern

Overview

This chapter will address the following issues:

- identifying causes for concern
- seeking help and advice from colleagues
- developing skills of observation
- understanding procedures
- supporting pupils and families.

Introduction

All teachers, including the most experienced, are from time to time confronted by a pupil who gives them some cause for concern. Sometimes the reason for this concern will be very clear, as when pupils are obviously having greater difficulties than their peers with learning. At other times, you will find greater difficulty in articulating exactly why you perceive that something is not right with a pupil in your class. Pupils fluctuate in their moods, their attitudes and their aptitudes for learning; this is to be expected and the same can be said of adults. As a teacher, you will quickly develop an understanding of the individuals in your class and should become adept at recognising when these variations are simply part of a normal pattern or something different that warrants extra attention.

Effective teachers are astute in their observation of pupils. They quickly learn to recognise symptoms of behaviour or attitude that are indicators that all is not well. As a new teacher, you may not always pick up on these signs and should be prepared to listen to colleagues around you who are possibly more familiar with individual pupils or more experienced as teachers.

Teaching assistants (TAs) who have worked with pupils over a number of years are sometimes more likely to detect signs that a pupil is having difficulties than you may be as a new teacher. It is important to make use of such expertise in order to ensure that you are able to provide maximum support to the pupils in your class. Early in your career, missing indicators that all is not well with an individual pupil may be regarded as acceptable. Ignoring the advice of more experienced colleagues is far less so.

Observation of pupils is an important skill that all teachers should continue to develop throughout their careers. Wragg (1999) has emphasised the difficulties which teachers face in becoming effective observers of pupils. Classrooms, he emphasises, are extremely busy places in which there is perpetual action and the teacher is confronted by an overwhelming number of tasks and responsibilities. Therefore, it is easy for even the most aware of teachers to overlook events or miss occurrences that may provide important evidence that an individual pupil is having some difficulty with learning. Furthermore, Wragg suggests that even when we become effective observers of pupils, we are confronted by a further challenge – that of interpretation of what we see. Whilst two experienced teachers may witness the same event, there is no guarantee that they will both interpret their observation in the same way, and this may ultimately influence any actions which follow. This should not deter you from making observations of pupils in order to ascertain whether they are making progress in accordance with expectations. Indeed, the observations of more than one adult can be useful even when interpretation does differ. This situation can often lead to helpful professional dialogue through which two colleagues can learn from each other and gain new insights into the pupil under consideration.

Quite naturally, many new teachers are particularly concerned to know what they should be looking for in order to identify pupils who may be at risk of failure in their classes. Much of this is a matter of common sense. Any significant change in a pupil's behaviour or mood, or sudden change in level of academic performance, should be noted. If this persists or deteriorates further, it may be a cause for concern rather than a passing phase and will need to be addressed. Assessment of pupils often begins in an informal manner with the observation that something is not quite right in a pupil's response to teaching. However, to gain useful and useable information about that pupil, this observation needs to be further developed in more formal ways in order to attain evidence upon which to base further teaching aimed at addressing problems.

Tilstone (1998) provides helpful guidelines with regard to the collection of evidence through observation. She calls upon teachers to be systematic in their approach and to develop strategies that allow for the consistent collection and interpretation of information about pupils. Tilstone provides us with a series of helpful examples of observation schedules to be used in a variety of situations and for different purposes. In so doing, she elucidates a number of critical features of effective classroom observation similar to those found in the works of other writers (Boehm and Weinberg, 1997; Sanger, 1996). Effective observation is generally dependent upon:

- a clear focus for the observation
- questions to which the observer is seeking answers
- identification of the most appropriate place to conduct the observation
- an effective means of recording
- forethought about how the observations will be used and analysed.

These principles can be best illustrated in the following case study.

Using observation

Harsha teaches a Year 4 class in a junior school. At the beginning of the school year, the pupils settled well, and they all appeared to be getting on well together. However, over the last few weeks, she has become concerned for Peter, a boy who has poor language skills and some difficulties with speech, and who appears to have become somewhat socially isolated in the class. Peter appears to have few friends, and when the class are given a choice about whom they want to work with, Peter often appears not to be chosen by others. Harsha fears that Peter's self-esteem may be affected by an increasing separation from his peers and that the class appear to be distancing themselves from him. She wants to improve the situation for Peter but does not want to cause difficulties for either him or his peers by insisting that he be included in specific class groups, as she is trying to encourage choice.

In order to make a decision about how to proceed, Harsha decides that she will make a series of observations of Peter in different situations. She decides to focus upon trying to ascertain if there are particular pupils who seem to relate better to Peter than others and to see if Peter chooses the company of specific pupils in the group. In order to do this, she observes Peter during the first session of each morning when pupils are encouraged to come into class and finish any leftover work from the previous day prior to registration. She also observes him on the playground at playtimes and in the school dining hall. After conducting observations during a 2-week period, Harsha discovers that in social situations Peter often works or plays alone, but that sometimes one of the other pupils from the class, Becky, spends time with him. Becky is a popular member of the class and has many friends.

At the end of her observations, Harsha decides upon a strategy to ensure that Peter is better included in classroom activities. For the early morning session, she tells all of the pupils in the class that before registration she wants them to check each other's work and to talk about what they did the previous day. She sorts the class into pairs and ensures that Peter and Becky are paired together. During registration, she asks each pupil to say one good thing about the work of the person with whom they were paired. In this way, Becky is encouraged to say something positive about Peter in a situation where all the class are able to hear.

Over the course of the next few weeks, the class become accustomed to this way of working and Harsha decides to change the classroom pairings now that Peter has developed more confidence in relating to one of his peers. She is

> careful to monitor this situation in order to ensure that Peter continues to participate effectively and to gauge whether he is becoming better accepted as a member of the class.

In this case study, we can see that Harsha has been effective in identifying a specific issue for a focus of her observations and has asked pertinent questions in order to address her concerns. She has identified appropriate times to conduct her observations and has made a commitment to action after the process. She does not see observation as the end product, but rather as a process whereby she can gain useful information which will influence her management of the class and hopefully the performance of an individual pupil who was giving her cause for concern.

As teachers become more experienced, they are better able to identify ways to address difficulties presented by individual pupils or groups. They often continue to use observation, but much of this becomes an internalised process, which is less dependent upon formal operations. As a new teacher, you are more likely to require the support which can be inherent in a structured observation procedure. By conducting observations and gathering evidence, you will accumulate knowledge and information, which you can then share with more experienced colleagues in order to benefit from their expertise. Many teachers, including those with several years of experience, comment on the value of classroom observation and often note that they see things that they had not anticipated through this process. Its value as part of your teaching armoury should never be underestimated.

Key questions and issues for reflection

- How do I currently gather evidence to address problems associated with individual pupils in my class?
- How might I develop my own skills of observation in order to assist my teaching?

Following procedures and taking actions in support of pupils giving cause for concern

You will be aware that when a pupil gives cause for concern in respect of learning or behaviour, there are set procedures which need to be followed in accordance with the SEN code of practice (DfES, 2001b). This code emphasises that the successful management of pupils with SEN is the responsibility of everyone within the school in collaboration with parents and other professional agencies. Your role as a new teacher is as important as that of any other individual in this process. This may appear to be a daunting responsibility, and indeed, the procedures that need to be followed can be onerous and exacting for all concerned. However, in well-organised schools, the procedures for assessment and identification of pupils with SEN are well established, and there will be colleagues who can support you in taking the correct actions. One of the mainstays of such support in schools will generally be the SENCO, with whom you should build a relationship as soon as possible after being appointed to a teaching post. SENCOs are generally experienced teachers who have a particular interest in the management and teaching of pupils with SEN. Many will have undertaken additional professional development, and possibly gained further accreditation in SEN. These professional colleagues can be an important source of support and advice for you; however, you will need to consider the pressures under which they often operate. The majority of SENCOs in primary schools are fulfilling this role in addition to their responsibilities as class teachers. If you are experiencing difficulties with or concerns about a pupil, you need to assist the SENCO by making the task of providing support easier. You can do this by making notes and collecting evidence about the pupil to share with the SENCO, making clear the exact nature of the difficulties being experienced. Being able to provide the SENCO with a clear description of the issues causing concern and also demonstrating the steps which you have already taken to address these will encourage the SENCO to see that you have taken a professional approach to your work and should be well received.

Being systematic in your approach to seeking support for a pupil giving cause for concern is important. As soon as you have concerns about a pupil, you should begin to keep detailed notes related to your worries. These should not only identify your cause for concern but also detail any interventions which you adopt to deal with this and the ways in which the pupil responds. By keeping these notes, you should be able to clarify the exact nature of the difficulty, not only for yourself, but also for the SENCO and anyone else who may become involved with the pupil. The notes should be maintained over a period of some weeks in order that you can establish any specific patterns in a pupil's behaviour or performance.

If the difficulties experienced by the pupil persist, you must inform the SENCO and ask for support. At this point, the SENCO may provide advice, come and observe the pupil, or conduct some form of assessment procedure. Here the notes which you have maintained will be vital in enabling appropriate actions or support to be provided quickly. The SENCO may be able to provide you with teaching ideas, resources or materials to help the pupil and should certainly be able to offer some advice. It is important that you implement any procedures required by the SENCO and keep your records of pupil responses to these interventions up-to-date. Sometimes a pupil may respond quickly to an appropriate action; on other occasions, the difficulties may persist. If the latter is the case, the SENCO may begin a process of assessment and may move to a formal procedure under the code of practice and place the pupil on 'school action'. Under the terms of the code of practice (DfES, 2001b,) school action is described as a procedure whereby the class teacher is required to provide interventions that are *additional to* or *different from* those provided as part of the school's usual differentiated curriculum and strategies (see code of practice, Chapter 5, para. 43). If the pupil is placed on school action, the SENCO will be responsible for overseeing any interventions implemented and for managing further assessments; however, it will be your responsibility as the class teacher to ensure that the procedures recommended by the SENCO are implemented with the pupil. In some instances, the SENCO may recommend that you receive some additional professional training, which could be related to the use of specialist equipment or techniques, in order to be more effective in supporting the pupil.

A pupil who is giving cause for concern and who is now at the stage of school action will require an individual education plan (IEP) to be constructed. In order to do this, it will be necessary to work closely with the SENCO, with the pupil's parents or carers, and with the pupil. The code of practice (DfES, 2001b) is very clear about the requirements for the contents of an IEP, which are as follows:

- the short-term targets set for or by the child
- the teaching strategies to be used
- the provision to be put in place
- when the plan is to be reviewed
- success and/or exit criteria
- outcomes (to be recorded when the IEP is reviewed). Code of Practice, P. 31, Para. 5.50)

Several writers (Farrell, 2003; Garner and Davies, 2001) have summarised the responsibilities of the class teacher when a pupil is on school action. The following case study provides an example of how this works in practice.

Supporting a pupil through school action

Toby teaches a Year 3 class in a primary school. In the autumn term, after a few weeks with a new class, he observes that one of his pupils, Gordon, appears to be struggling with his work in many of the lessons. Whilst Gordon is generally an articulate and cooperative pupil during some lessons, he seems very distracted and at times disrupts the learning of others. Toby feels that he is perpetually reminding Gordon to get on with his work and needs to intervene regularly in order to keep him on task. He is also conscious of the fact that he is often using an inordinate amount of the TA's time in supporting Gordon.

Toby has kept records of Gordon's progress and makes notes based upon a number of observations. Within a fairly short time, it becomes apparent that Gordon is not making good progress and that he is beginning to fall behind his peers in many aspects of learning. Toby decides to seek the advice of the school's SENCO, Angela. She looks at Toby's records and samples of Gordon's work and discusses these with Toby. Angela agrees that Gordon is giving cause for concern and that his records provide helpful evidence to support this. Together, Toby and Angela plan a way forward for supporting Toby's teaching and to encourage improved performance from Gordon. Angela spends a little time in Toby's class observing Gordon and recording how he responds to a range of teaching situations. She notes that Gordon is easily distracted and that his concentration appears limited in some lessons.

Toby and Angela construct an IEP which identifies as a main target improving attention and concentration on tasks set in lessons. Together, they plan how to do this and agree on the following interventions.

In maths lessons, which appear to be particularly problematic for Gordon, when working individually, he will be located alongside two of the most able pupils in the class who concentrate well and tend to work efficiently. At the beginning of the session, the TA will settle Gordon and ensure that he knows what is expected of him. She will tell him that if he works steadily for 5 minutes without disrupting other pupils he will be allowed 5 minutes where he can choose another activity. After this, he must go back to his work for a further 5 minutes. Toby provides a timer so that Gordon will know when his 5-minute period is completed.

Toby implements this intervention with Gordon, who, after a few days, begins to respond well. Other pupils appear pleased with this arrangement, as disruption of their work has been considerably decreased. Toby keeps careful records and discusses the progress which Gordon is making with him and with the SENCO. After just 4 weeks, there is a noticeable improvement, and Toby decides to lengthen gradually the time which he expects Gordon to remain on task. At the end of a term, Toby and Angela review progress with Gordon and his mother. They all agree that his work has improved and his concentration has been helped by the intervention. However, they decide to continue with the action for the following term in order to ensure that progress is sustained.

In this case study, we can see that improvement in Gordon's performance was dependent upon collaboration between Toby, Angela, Gordon and his mother. In this instance, success was achieved and life became easier for everyone in the class. This was achieved only because Toby was well organised in maintaining records and conducting observations, reflected upon what he had learned about Gordon, consulted with Angela and put an appropriate intervention into place. Whilst this intervention resulted in a successful outcome, you should not necessarily expect that success will always be so easily gained. Often, you will need to experiment with different approaches or a range of resources to find solutions to the problems of learning experienced by pupils. The advice of the SENCO and your ability to respond are clearly important here. It will continue to be so if the pupil fails to make satisfactory progress and decisions are made to move through the next stage of the code of practice referred to as 'school action plus'.

School action plus comes into play if a pupil continues to present concerns despite interventions or procedures implemented through school action. Often at school action plus, professional colleagues from other agencies may become more directly involved with a pupil. At this phase of intervention, you will need to continue to act on the advice of the SENCO but may also find yourself more directly involved with other agencies for which you will need to have a set of working principles. The ways in which you engage with your professional colleagues are important not only for maintaining good working relationships, but also in respect of providing effective support for pupils. Principles of working with professional colleagues are addressed throughout this book. However, early in your career, you are strongly advised to take advice from the SENCO and other school managers.

Key questions and issues for reflection

- How conversant am I with the school's SEN policy and the procedures for assessment and support of pupils?
- What expectations does the school SENCO have of me, and how can I ensure that I provide appropriate information as requested?
- Are there examples of IEPs written for other pupils in the school that can provide me with guidance on school expectations?

Working with colleagues from other agencies

In Chapter 6 we discuss the importance of being part of an effective, inclusive classroom team. This includes establishing a working partnership with professional colleagues from a range of agencies. The move toward a more collaborative approach to supporting young people through the development of integrated children's services involving professionals from health and social services as well as education, and the introduction of initiatives such as 'extended schools', means that, in future, provision for the support of all pupils will be managed in a far more collaborative way than has often characterised previous actions. The importance of such collaboration is particularly clear when considering the ways in which pupils with SEN are supported.

When pupils receive support at school action plus they often receive assessment or intervention from professionals from a variety of agencies. These may be health professionals, such as speech therapists or physiotherapists; colleagues from social services; or others, such as psychologists or members of education support services. As a teacher, you will be responsible for providing such colleagues with information and may be required to implement programmes provided by them. Each profession has its own expectations, procedures and jargon, and it is important that you understand something about the ways in which your professional colleagues operate. Lacey (2001) talks about the necessity to develop a shared culture between professionals from different services. She suggests that whilst teachers, therapists or social workers may all come from different disciplines, they share a common concern for the development and progress of young people. This common interest must be used to overcome professional differences and provide benefits for pupils. As a new teacher, you may at times find yourself working with colleagues who see things from a different perspective from your own. You should see this as an opportunity to learn and to broaden your own appreciation of different ways of working with pupils, rather than taking a more narrowly focused view based only upon your own professional training. You should never lack the confidence to ask for clarification of procedures or an explanation of terminology with which you may be unfamiliar. You will also find that these colleagues depend upon you, as someone who works with a pupil on a daily basis, to provide information and insights that they are otherwise unable to obtain. The SENCO should support you when working with colleagues from other agencies, particularly if you are required to undertake work using materials, programmes or approaches provided by them.

A set of principles to support you in your work with colleagues from other agencies is important. You will find it is far more beneficial for both you and the pupils for whom you have concern if you

- gain a clear understanding of the roles and responsibilities of professional colleagues from other agencies
- share your own professional experiences and expertise, and provide information which your colleagues cannot readily obtain
- maintain records which are free from jargon and clearly written
- implement any programmes or interventions provided by professional colleagues.

There is much we can learn from working with colleagues from other disciplines. Often, if pupils are giving cause for concern, it is essential that they receive support from a professional who has certain skills, knowledge and understanding that most teachers do not have. You should not feel in any way inadequate in this situation but rather see this as an opportunity to broaden your own understanding of how pupils can best be supported.

Supporting families through assessment procedures

When pupils give cause for concern, you will understandably have some worries about how you are to address their needs. It is important to remember that, whilst you may have anxieties about this situation for the pupils concerned and their families, this is likely to be a period of some stress. Both pupils and their families require you to provide appropriate support through processes of assessment. Carpenter (2005) has written of the anxieties, fears and apprehensions that many families experience when they first receive news that their child may have some form of SEN. Whilst, for teachers, the language of special education has become accepted as a common focus of discussion in schools, this is a highly personal and worrying issue for families. As a teacher, you must be able to empathise with the stresses which families experience when going through periods of assessment or discussions which identify their children as having any kind of difficulty.

Pupils themselves are often aware that they are having difficulties. They will compare their own academic and social performance to that of their peers and make their own judgement about how they are progressing. If pupils become aware that they are having difficulties, they may react in any of a number of ways. Some will approach you and ask for help; others will experience feelings of failure or inadequacy and may become distant or withdrawn. In some instances, poor behaviour can be directly attributed to academic performance, pupils venting their frustration at being unable to succeed. It is important that you recognise a range of reactions but more particularly that pupils see you as supportive and prepared to involve them fully in addressing their needs.

When formal assessment procedures begin for a pupil with SEN, you will need to provide additional support to the pupil concerned. Pupils can become anxious when they are visited by professionals with titles such as psychologist or therapist and may be unsure as to the role of these colleagues or why they are paying them so much attention. You will possibly be the only professional adult with whom the pupil has had an opportunity to develop a stable relationship. Furthermore, you will see the pupil more often than any visiting professional and will therefore more likely be seen as someone to whom the pupil can turn with some confidence. Your support for a pupil can make a huge difference not only to their confidence, but also to the success of any intervention by your professional colleagues.

You must establish well-defined working practices to support pupils who are going through assessment in respect of potential SEN. If you know that pupils are to be visited by a professional colleague, you should prepare them for this visit by talking to them about who is coming, what they might expect and why they are being seen. Most importantly, you need to reassure them that they are not being seen because they have done something wrong but rather that this is part of a process of helping you to work better with them. The following case study illustrates how one teacher provided effective support for a pupil who after a period at school action was being assessed though school action plus.

In this case study, we can see how Lois has attempted to demonstrate to Hannah that there is nothing to worry about from the visit of the educational psychologist. The management of this situation necessitated Lois having a discussion with the educational psychologist before the visit to ensure that he spent time in class talking to other pupils rather than singling out Hannah as being in need of all his attention. In this way, the other pupils saw the educational psychologist as an interesting visitor and probably felt that Hannah was fortunate in being selected for particular attention. The time spent with Hannah by Lois both before and after the visit was essential in enabling Hannah to feel comfortable with what happened and in providing support on a personal level.

Supporting a pupil through a visit by the educational psychologist

Hannah, a Year 1 pupil, has been having difficulties with learning in most subjects for the past year. The school has implemented a number of programmes to assist her, but her teacher fears that she is getting further behind the rest of the class in both English and mathematics, and that she also has difficulty making friends and maintaining relationships. The school has asked for an assessment by an educational psychologist, who will visit Hannah in school next week. Lois, Hannah's teacher, talks to Hannah about the visit and tells her that the educational psychologist is a friend of hers and will be coming to see Hannah and to talk to both of them about how they work together in class. Lois emphasises that the educational psychologist is coming to help her rather than to focus upon Hannah.

On the day of the visit, Lois tells all of the class that a visitor is coming to see them all working together in class, and that he may want to talk to some of the pupils. When the educational psychologist arrives, after discussion with Lois, he spends some time in class talking to several of the pupils and looking at their work. He then works with Hannah to conduct his assessments.

After the visit, Lois talks to the whole class, saying how impressed the visitor had been with them and how much he had enjoyed his visit. She makes time to see Hannah and talk about the things which Hannah had been asked to do, offering her praise for her work with the visitor. She explains that the educational psychologist will be giving some ideas of other things that she will be able to do to help Hannah in class.

Just as pupils need support, so might it be necessary for you to maintain regular contact with parents or carers through a period of intensive assessment or intervention. Here, you must take advice from the senior managers in your school. Different parents or carers will require varying levels of support. When pupils give cause for concern, the school will need to make contact with the parents as soon as possible. This can be a worrying time for parents, and it is important that both accurate and carefully expressed information is provided. As a new teacher, you are strongly advised to consult with the SENCO or senior school managers when dealing with parents in this situation. You are also advised to keep written records of any contact that you have with parents recording any concerns expressed and any actions taken.

Parents will often see you as their main point of contact with the school. In some instances, if they bring their children to school, they may have daily contact with you and come to know you quite well and to trust you as a professional friend. This has advantages for them in being able to talk about their child in a fairly relaxed manner but can also be a source of some difficulty if you are not always cautious about what you say. Parents will often seek reassurance about a child who is going through assessment of SEN from a teacher in whom they have confidence. It is important that you offer this support, but that you are both honest and discreet. A few rules will assist you in ensuring that you support parents effectively.

- Never talk to parents about their children's needs or difficulties where the pupil concerned will overhear.
- Never talk about the pupil in the hearing of other parents.
- Avoid using jargon.
- Listen carefully to any anxieties or questions expressed by parents and do not offer hasty responses or solutions.
- When you cannot provide answers to parent questions, admit this and say that you will find out from someone else – after making this promise, ensure that it is kept.
- Make a record of conversations which express concerns about pupils.
- Make sure that parents are informed about any potential visits by other professionals to their child.
- Consult with the SENCO about any concerns expressed by parents.
- Be honest when asked about pupil progress but use language that expresses your interest in the pupil and demonstrates that you are working to achieve positive outcomes.
- Be aware of and sensitive to the anxieties which parents or carers may feel about their child and which may affect their response to you as the teacher.

As a new teacher, you should receive support and guidance from the management of the school at all stages of the identification and management of pupils with SEN. This should include guidance on relating to and supporting parents. When pupils are undergoing assessment and a school has expressed concerns about their learning, it is inevitable that this will cause some stresses for all concerned. An important part of your professional role is that of minimising this stress and providing appropriate support to both pupils and families.

Key questions and issues for reflection:

- How do I support pupils going through periods of assessment of SEN?
- What support can I expect from the SENCO and school managers in communicating to parents about SEN?
- What kind of records should I keep with regard to the feelings of pupils and parents going through assessment?
- What does the school expect of me in working closely with parents?

Conclusion

All teachers experience times when they are challenged by the learning or behaviour difficulties that they encounter in their classrooms. As you gain more experience, you will become more confident in identifying potential difficulties and planning to address them. It is vital that you identify sources of support in school that can enable you to address the needs of pupils more effectively. This will include the SENCO and other more experienced teachers with whom you work. The school will have policies relating to SEN which detail how you should proceed in relation to the requirements of the SEN code of practice. It is important that you become familiar with this document and adhere to its procedures. It is equally important that you gain an understanding of the roles and responsibilities of other professional colleagues who may be involved with pupils in your class.

Working with families requires skills and understanding that are not quickly attained. Parents and carers will invest trust in you that you must repay by respecting their role and understanding the challenges which they may face in accepting and understanding their child with SEN. Above all other responsibilities, your main function is to provide support to the pupils in your class. Their dignity must be upheld and their needs met wherever possible by you as an adult whom they trust to have their interests at heart. Recognising that having SEN is a challenge for the pupil as well as for you as the teacher, is a critical stage in becoming an effective teacher.

4 Teaching and learning

Overview

This chapter will address the following issues:

- teaching and learning styles
- teaching and learning: pupils with special educational needs (SEN)
- specialist strategies or inclusive strategies?
- structured teaching
- multisensory teaching
- management of group work
- jigsawing.

Introduction

How do teachers teach and how do pupils learn? Effective education depends to some extent upon careful consideration of these two questions. Much has been written about teaching and learning styles (e.g. Read, 1998; Riding and Cheema, 1991; Smith, 1996), yet, frequently, the answers to these questions remain challenging. As a newly qualified teacher, or a teacher developing expertise in teaching pupils with SEN, you will need to consider both how you teach and the range of teaching strategies available to you, at the same time questioning how individual pupils learn best. Inclusive classrooms will inevitably require teachers to draw upon an eclectic range of teaching strategies in order to *respond to diverse learning needs* and to *overcome potential barriers to learning and assessment* (DfEE/QCA, 1999). This chapter focuses upon issues relating to teaching and learning, suggesting strategies for self-reflection in this area. A selection of so-called specialist strategies commonly used to promote teaching and learning for pupils with SEN will be explored, examining how they may be implemented to benefit many pupils (including those who do not have SEN) and how to manage them in inclusive classroom environments. These strategies are by no means exhaustive, but serve to provide illustrations of how 'specialist' strategies can be incorporated effectively into inclusive practice for the benefit of all.

It is important to remember that pupils learn in different ways and will develop preferred learning styles and that teachers develop preferred teaching styles. Inclusive classrooms demand flexible and diverse teaching practices in order to meet effectively the diverse learning needs of individual learners. Effective planning and differentiation will depend in part upon the teacher's ability to match teaching styles and activities to pupils' learning styles in order to develop strengths and to motivate all learners. Smith (1996) suggests that learning is most effective when experiences are presented through preferred learning 'modalities', naming the three key learning styles as visual, auditory and kinaesthetic. However, this may lead teachers to believe, for example, that a visual learner should have all teaching activities presented in visual ways. This approach may in reality limit the pupil's opportunities to develop experiences and skills through different modalities; therefore, as Hume (2005) reminds us, *teaching needs to contain elements of all three learning styles.*

Whilst it is important to identify individuals' preferred learning styles, this should not limit the experiences and opportunities available to children. Coffield et al. (2004) suggest that labelling pupils with a particular learning style can restrict learning. Teachers may need to think about creating opportunities for individuals to learn through their preferred learning modality and to develop skills and experiences in other modalities. This view is echoed in the work of Gardner (1983; 1993; 1999), who has identified various 'intelligences': linguistic, logical-mathematical, spatial, musical, bodily kinaesthetic, interpersonal, intrapersonal, naturalist and existentialist. Gardner suggests that each learner will have a unique cognitive profile of learning intelligences, and that classroom experiences should provide opportunities for individuals to develop skills in all areas, rather than limit experiences to those presented through the pupil's preferred learning modality only. Kornhaber et al. (2004) present a range of examples of schools' approaches in the USA to promoting multiple intelligences. One such example illustrates how an activity involving pupils in writing book reviews was successfully managed to enable individual pupils to *take on roles that engage them through their strengths and expose them to their weaknesses* (p131). Pupils were organised into 'book clubs' with each pupil in a group of four allocated a role or 'job'. Initially, all pupils were assigned to a job according to their strengths. However, as the book club reviewed more books, the jobs were rotated, providing opportunities for individuals to try out more challenging work after observing how others might have tackled the task. Kornhaber et al. (2004) suggest that this approach enables pupils to *engage through their strengths; in this way their talents are recognized, and their learning needs are addressed* (p131).

As classrooms and schools strive to become inclusive and more effective in meeting the needs of all pupils, so teaching and learning require a reflective approach. Teachers have a responsibility to develop an understanding of how individual pupils learn, as Read (1998) suggests:

> If pupils are disadvantaged by inappropriate teaching and learning styles, by a failure to develop an understanding of how individuals learn most effectively, they become the recipient of a 'compound deficit model' of learning and disadvantage. (p136)

Shaw and Hawes (1998) also discuss the implications of learning styles for classroom practice, suggesting that teachers need to bring learning strategies into 'conscious awareness', making them explicit in teaching. Addressing teaching and learning styles is not about providing all learning experience through preferred learning modalities; rather, it is about providing diverse experiences and opportunities for pupils to develop strengths and to develop skills and experiences across the 'intelligences'.

Teaching and learning: pupils with SEN

If we accept that all pupils will learn in different ways and that teachers have a responsibility to provide opportunities for pupils to develop strengths and to address individual learning needs through the whole range of learning styles and intelligences, it becomes clear that this approach is equally relevant to all pupils, including those who have SEN. As with all pupils, those with SEN will learn in different ways, will develop preferred learning styles, will have strengths and will have individual learning needs, all of which lead to a unique cognitive profile. Effective teaching will ensure that all pupils are provided with opportunities for learning, using all learning intelligences. The following description of needs associated with ASD illustrates how the cognitive profile of pupils with SEN needs to be considered in order to develop effective teaching and learning.

ASD: individual needs

The individual needs of pupils with ASD are well documented and include core challenges in the area of the triad of impairments; that is communication; social interaction; and repetitive and restricted behaviours, activities and interests (Wing and Gould, 1979). Pupils with ASD will also face challenges in other areas, including short-term working memory, attention, organisation, sequencing and problem-solving, which may limit their opportunities to access the curriculum (Jordan and Powell, 1990; Mesibov and Howley, 2003). Some argue that different cognitive processes in pupils with ASD lead to different ways of thinking. For example, Frith (1989) suggests that weak central coherence affects thinking styles, due to difficulties integrating detail in order to interpret the 'whole picture'; this may lead to problems with discriminating between relevant, important detail and irrelevant detail. DeClerq (2003) provides numerous examples of her son's 'detailed thinking' style to illustrate this difference. Peeters (1997) and Powell (2000) focus upon the resultant difficulties pupils with ASD may have with extracting and interpreting meaning. If we consider this in relation to the classroom, traditional teaching strategies, founded upon language, communication and interaction, may prove meaningless for the pupil with ASD. Powell (2000) suggests that problems with understanding meaning have a number of implications for learning, including a reliance upon rote memory, difficulties with prediction, difficulties making connections between events and learning, and difficulties with categorisation. Differences in thinking styles have significant implications for teaching and learning; pupils with ASD will think, and therefore learn, in different ways from the majority of pupils in the classroom. As a consequence, pupils with ASD may experience the classroom, teaching and learning quite differently from other pupils.

In addition to understanding areas of challenge for pupils with ASD, teachers must take into account strengths and abilities. For example, people with ASD are thought to perform better on visual search tasks due to superior visual discrimination ability (e.g. O'Riordan et al. 2001; O'Riordan and Plaisted, 2001). Personal accounts provided by people with ASD support this view. For example, Grandin (1995) explains: *I think in pictures. Words are like a second language to me ... When somebody speaks to me, his words are instantly translated into pictures* (p19).

This strength can frequently be used to help to compensate for areas that may be challenging for pupils with ASD and the strategy may be useful in facilitating both teaching and learning by utilising visual structure to enhance meaning. Effective teaching and learning for pupils with ASD will therefore need to consider and address issues relating to meaning, differences in thinking styles, interpersonal learning and the use of visual strategies to enhance meaning and independence. Failure to address these differences may well lead to dependence upon familiar adults who interpret the classroom 'culture' and emphasis upon behaviour-management strategies rather than on teaching and learning.

This description of needs in ASD illustrates the importance of developing knowledge and understanding about individual needs and indicates the professional development responsibility of all teachers to learn about specific disorders and teaching approaches that may be recommended for pupils with particular needs. Knowledge and understanding of individual needs and specific teaching strategies need to be integral to classroom practice, including all aspects of planning and teaching. This is challenging and may seem daunting; hence, this chapter explores how teaching and learning opportunities for pupils with SEN can be managed in inclusive classrooms.

Specialist strategies or inclusive strategies?

In response to the diverse range of needs and strengths of all pupils, it has become clear that teaching styles and strategies need to be equally diverse.

Special schools frequently employ a range of teaching strategies to meet a range of needs, and many of these approaches are now becoming established in inclusive classrooms. Furthermore, the government's strategy for SEN (DfES, 2004b) indicates a commitment to developing teaching strategies in inclusive classrooms by developing *a framework of evidence-based strategies and teaching approaches* to help teachers meet diverse and individual needs. The rest of this chapter examines three teaching approaches, structured teaching, multisensory teaching and jigsawing, which are commonly used with pupils with SEN, to illustrate how such approaches may be incorporated and managed in inclusive classrooms. Whilst the examples provided are focused upon pupils with specific diagnoses of SEN, it is important to consider the principles under consideration and their application to a wide range of learners.

Structured teaching

Structured teaching is one component of the approach called 'treatment and education for autistic and related communication handicapped children' (TEACCH), devised at the University of North Carolina at Chapel Hill in the 1970s and now used in classrooms in the UK and worldwide. The approach has *evolved as a way of matching educational practices to the different ways that people with ASD understand, think, and learn* and provides *a system of organising the classroom and making teaching processes autism-friendly*. (Mesibov and Howley, 2003, p8). Structured teaching comprises four elements: physical structure (see Chapter 5), visual schedules, work (organisational) systems and additional visual information that adds clarification and visual instructions to supplement verbal directions. An essential feature of the approach is the emphasis upon the use of visual structure and information in the classroom to support learning and to enhance meaning. Structured teaching is underpinned by key principles that include:

- Assessment of individual needs: the approach requires an *in-depth knowledge and understanding of the unique characteristics of each individual* including assessment of strengths and weaknesses, likes/dislikes, motivational factors and visual cognition.
- Development of individualised structure, comprising all four elements of the approach, according to assessed individual needs and taking into account idiosyncratic learning profiles.
- An emphasis upon developing independence, self-esteem and effective behaviour management strategies, including self-management.
- Enhanced meaning within the learning context (Howley, 2006).

Whilst the approach has been developed to meet the individual learning needs of pupils with ASD, taking into account differences in social and communication skills, thinking styles and motivational factors, the approach has also been shown to be applicable and manageable in inclusive settings. Howley and Kime (2003) provide examples of how the approach can be utilised within inclusive classrooms, with benefits both for the individual and for other learners. Mesibov and Howley (2003) also provide examples of inclusive practice within each component of the approach. Three elements of the approach, schedules, work systems and visual structure, are considered here in relation to their use in inclusive classrooms and how they may benefit all learners. Physical structure is considered in Chapter 5.

Schedules

The provision of timetable information for all pupils is easily adapted to provide individualised schedules for pupils with ASD. The use of objects, pictures or symbol cues can enhance the meaning of written words provided on the class timetable. Moreover, the introduction of a visual schedule for a pupil with ASD has been shown to have advantages for the whole class, icons and symbols enhancing timetable meaning for emergent readers (DfEE, 2000). The 'order of the day', often written on whiteboards for the class, can be individualised for pupils with ASD to enhance meaning for them. Figure 4.1 illustrates how a visual schedule can enhance the written class timetable.

| numeracy | snack | playtime | literacy | choose |

Figure 4.1 Individualised schedule using icons and symbols to enhance meaning. Boardmaker™ is a trademark of Mayer-Johnson LLC.

The use of individualised schedules can provide strategies for addressing a range of individual needs. For example, Figure 4.2 shows a schedule that incorporates pupils' interests, at the same time encouraging participation in activities beyond their interest.

| music | dinosaurs | art | dinosaurs | playtime |

Figure 4.2 Individualised schedule incorporating interest. Boardmaker™ is a trademark of Mayer-Johnson LLC.

The use of visual schedules improves the teacher's communication to pupils with ASD, helping pupils to understand the sequence of activities and lessons, and to make sense of the seemingly chaotic school day. Schedules can also be extended for some, providing opportunities for pupils to make choices, and to develop decision-making and problem-solving skills (Mesibov and Howley, 2003). Schedules can therefore be used in various ways to meet individual needs within an inclusive classroom, derived from the class order of the day and developed to provide specific information, in a specific visual format, for individual pupils according to their needs. This strategy can be used for individual pupils in a class with a variety of learning needs, including non-readers and pupils with other SEN who would benefit from individualised timetable information. For example, Howley and Preece (2003) discuss how the approach can be adapted for pupils with visual impairments. Other visual learners may also benefit from the approach, such as pupils with Down's syndrome or those with learning difficulties.

Key questions and issues for reflection

- How do I present the <u>class</u> timetable? Is the information accessible to all? Can additional visual cues enhance meaning and be more inclusive?
- How do <u>individuals</u> know what will be happening, where and when?
- How are pupils prepared for changes to the timetable?

Work systems

Structured teaching makes use of 'work systems' that provide organisational strategies for pupils with ASD. As with the schedule, careful assessment of individual needs leads to the development of individualised systems that help the pupil to develop organisational strategies. Poor executive functioning (Ozonoff, 1995) can result in pupils with ASD experiencing difficulties with organisation, planning and sequencing. This may result in an over focus upon trying to organise resources, time and verbal directions, rather than focusing upon the learning task and objectives. Individualised organisational strategies should provide pupils with information that enables them to be better organised, alleviating anxiety about lack of organisation and reducing adult dependence. Work systems answer key questions for the pupil: What do I have to do? How much do I have to do? How am I progressing? What do I do with finished (and unfinished) work? What will I do next? Often information relating to these questions is presented to the class through verbal directions. This means, however, that pupils with ASD, may not respond appropriately due to lack of understanding of language, poor short-term memory for verbal directions and problems recalling the sequence of instructions. These challenges are not unique to pupils with ASD; indeed, pupils with other SEN may face similar challenges (e.g. pupils with speech and language disorders, pupils with attention deficit, pupils with learning difficulties and pupils with dyslexia). The consideration of providing organisational strategies in different formats may prove useful for a number of pupils in the classroom. Work systems are developed to answer these key questions by providing the information required in different formats, depending upon individual needs; systems include basic left-to right/motoric work systems, sequenced 'to do' lists and written organisation systems (Kunce and Mesibov, 1998; Schopler et al., 1995). The use of work systems might therefore enable pupils with ASD, and other pupils with SEN to organise themselves more effectively. For example, pupils in early years settings may benefit from basic left-to-right organisation systems through which they learn to locate their work (perhaps on a shelf to their left), complete tasks, put completed work away (perhaps on a shelf on their right) and move to their next activity. More independent pupils may be able to use numbered 'to do' lists or follow written sequences of instructions which they check off to keep track of their progress (Figure 4.3).

Maths lesson

1. Whole class – listen   ☑

2. Pentagons group – maths book 3, pages 45 and 46   ☑

3. Maths activity on computer   ☑

4. Whole class – listen   ☑

Figure 4.3 Written organisation system. Boardmaker™ is a trademark of Mayer-Johnson LLC.

Mesibov and Howley (2003) provide numerous examples of how work systems can be used within a range of settings. Inclusive strategies for organisation can also be used effectively for the whole class; these include specific locations for pupils to put finished and unfinished work, provision of a basket of resources required for an activity on the table of a pupil who is disorganised, ensuring resources are labelled with additional visual cues for emergent readers, and placing visual reminders of verbal instructions at each group table.

Key questions and issues for reflection

- Are resources organised and labelled so that <u>all</u> pupils can locate them?
- Can I introduce organisational strategies for the class; such as 'finished' and 'unfinished' trays or boxes?

- Are sequences of instructions at the beginning of lessons accessible to <u>all</u> pupils? How are these instructions presented? How can pupils recall them during the lesson?
- Can I consider organisational strategies for activities outside the classroom such as PE, playtimes?

Visual structure

The final component of structured teaching considers the use of visual information to clarify meaning and to supplement verbal directions. Pupils with ASD are disadvantaged when teachers present information through verbal language only. Visual processing abilities are frequently superior to auditory ones, and pupils who do have apparently good understanding of verbal language may still process visual directions more efficiently. Visual information can be incorporated into lessons and tasks to enhance the meaning of the activity. Mesibov and Howley (2003) provide examples of how visual structure can enhance meaning and be used as an effective differentiation strategy. The addition of visual cues and information serves to help the pupil with ASD make sense of the meaning of abstract and confusing verbal language by <u>showing</u> what we mean. Strategies might include the use of pictures or icons and symbols (Figure 4.4), prepared topic vocabularies, visual cue cards, written reminders, highlighting key information on worksheets, diagrams and so on.

Figure 4.4 Visual cues used in a PE lesson. Boardmaker™ is a trademark of Mayer-Johnson LLC.

The 'fading' of some visual cues, perhaps introducing a question mark, may encourage some to begin to develop their own thinking and to solve problems. These strategies, as with the other elements of structured teaching, can be used effectively in inclusive settings for the benefits of pupils with ASD but can also be effective for pupils with other SEN. For example, Brower and Barber (2005) describe how visual supports are helpful to pupils with language and communication difficulties. Similarly, pupils with learning difficulties, poor short-term working memory for verbal directions and/or hearing impairments may benefit from the use of visual structure and instructions to supplement verbal language in the classroom.

> ### Key questions and issues for reflection
>
> - Can I differentiate by adding visual cues and information to supplement verbal directions and explanations?
> - Can pupils 'see' what I mean?

Structured teaching is a widely used teaching strategy for pupils with ASD. This individualised approach is not, however, exclusive to pupils with ASD. Pupils with other SEN, and indeed others who have no specific difficulties, may benefit from (visual) structure and consideration of the four elements of structured teaching within classroom organisation, and lesson planning may enhance teaching and learning for all pupils. Furthermore, the approach does not demand that all teaching be restricted to visual teaching styles for visual learners. For example, a multisensory 'story time' may be accessed more readily for some pupils if supported by visual structure (their strength) in order to develop skills in weaker areas such as listening. This approach to utilising a 'specialist' strategy may lead to more effective teaching and learning by providing a visual structure for pupils who are visual learners in order to scaffold and support learning through multiple intelligences and sensory modalities.

Multisensory teaching

Multisensory approaches to teaching are inextricably linked to our knowledge of the brain and the potential for learning. Shaw and Hawes (1998) suggest that *learning is the process of neurons making connections* (p9) and provide a readable account of the structure of the brain and its functions. In particular, they outline the implications of the division of the brain into two hemispheres: the left, analytical hemisphere overseeing language, logic, number concepts and sequential working; the right, intuitive hemisphere being concerned with the non-verbal, visualisation, imagination, rhyme and rhythm. Pupils will develop hemisphere dominance, leading to preferred learning styles and personal approaches to learning tasks; equally, teachers' hemisphere dominance will influence their teaching styles. However, as Shaw and Hawes (1998) point out, *the most effective thinking and learning can take place when both sides of the brain are working in harmony together* (p23). They further suggest that teachers should offer activities and provide opportunities that will stimulate both sides of the brain, providing the example of using music to promote learning, combining harmony (right brain) with words (left brain).

This theory is applicable to all learners and has direct relevance to pupils with particular SEN. For example, the neurobiological basis of dyslexia or ASD has significant implications for the ways in which pupils with dyslexia or ASD may learn. The identification of preferred learning styles, based upon brain functioning, is essential in order to match teaching styles to learning styles, and Exley (2005) suggests, for example, that pupils with dyslexia can improve their performance and self-esteem if encouraged to use their preferred learning styles; However, teaching approaches should not be restricted exclusively to preferred learning styles; indeed, teachers perhaps should consider how they plan and teach activities that provide opportunities for pupils to utilise a range of intelligences and sensory modalities in order make good use of personal strengths and to develop skills in weaker areas, as, for example, in the approaches described above of Kornhaber et al. (2004).

Multisensory approaches to teaching may well provide teachers with a useful strategy for ensuring that pupils are provided with opportunities for learning that combine left and right brain activity. Ott (1997) defines multisensory teaching as *the simultaneous use of the eyes, ears, hands and lips to utilize all the pathways to the brain when learning* (p8). This approach is embedded within the Foundation Stage curriculum (DfEE/QCA, 2000) and the philosophy of the National Literacy Strategy (DfEE, 1998), with an emphasis on building on strengths and at the same time reducing weaknesses. Multisensory teaching is relevant to all pupils and has specific benefits for pupils with dyslexia and other specific learning difficulties. Multisensory approaches to teaching literacy encourage learning through all sensory channels. For example, the use of tactile letters, so that pupils can feel the letter at the same time as looking at its shape, may be helpful in early letter recognition; 'sky-writing' incorporates movement within learning; singing common spellings may help some pupils with recall. A variety of multisensory strategies should therefore be utilised to help pupils to recall their learning. To demonstrate learning, children have to recall information that has been stored in their memory. For a child who has difficulty 'remembering' what has been taught, 'memory cues' can facilitate this process. These memory cues should be something that links what has to be recalled with something already learned. For example, the teaching of vowel digraphs is often potentially confusing for some pupils; digraphs should ideally be taught separately, to avoid confusion, and different multisensory strategies used to support memory and recall. For example, in teaching 'ea', letter-shaped biscuits can be used by pupils to build words containing 'ea' that they can then <u>eat</u>; when learning spellings with 'ee', pupils can be asked to draw pictures that illustrate relevant words (see the following case study)[1].

[1] Multisensory examples were kindly provided by Liz Waine, Centre for Special Needs Education and Research (CeSNER), University of Northampton.

> ## Memory cue for 'ee' words
>
> When his class were focusing on the long phoneme /e/, Connor's teacher chose the 'ee' words from the literacy strategy as his spelling target.
>   Connor knew how to spell 'queen', so this was included in his list of words. For a child to learn, he has first to attend to the teaching. Connor was passionate about cars, so the word 'jeep' was included to ensure his attention.
>   Connor linked these words to make the sentence *I can see a queen in a jeep between three green trees*. He then illustrated this sentence (Figure 4.5). Every time he had to spell one of the 'ee' words from his list, he was helped to recall the picture and sentence to reinforce the memory cue. This ensured that the teaching was fully multisensory: Connor looked at the words and listened to himself as he spelt out each word, he wrote them down at word level and in a sentence, he drew a picture, he looked at the picture and repeated the sentence, and recalled the spelling of the words.

Figure 4.5 Multisensory approaches: memory cue for 'ee'. Boardmaker™ is a trademark of Mayer-Johnson LLC.

The benefits of multisensory approaches are not restricted to teaching literacy. Ott (1997) provides examples of multisensory teaching methods for teaching mathematics, suggesting the need for pupils to work with concrete objects and to verbalise what they are doing. Multisensory teaching for pupils with sensory impairments and/or learning difficulties may also enable teachers to provide stimulating opportunities for learning and participation. For example, Bishop and Jones (2005) report on the experiences of early years teacher-training students and the development of science teaching for pupils with severe and profound learning difficulties. Science-based activities that supported scientific learning through multisensory approaches were found to be effective in keeping children on task for considerable lengths of time and in allowing pupils to demonstrate higher levels of understanding than expected. Multisensory approaches offer opportunities for pupils to engage in activities that promote left and right brain functioning. Pupils' preferred learning styles can be utilised effectively, at the same time providing opportunities for strengthening weaker channels. For example, visual learners, such as those with ASD or Down's syndrome, may find that the use of visual cues enables them to begin to integrate visual information with spoken language which may be helpful when learning to read (Tod Broun, 2004).

Multisensory approaches should be integral to all planning and embedded within classroom practice. In this way, all pupils are encouraged to learn in a variety of ways, to recall their learning and to enjoy their learning – multisensory approaches should be fun, and therefore learning in this way is more likely to be retained and generalised.

Key questions and issues for reflection

- Am I aware of the preferred learning styles of individual pupils?
- Am I aware of my own preferred learning and teaching styles? (Shaw and Hawes, 1998, provide useful questionnaires (pp128–31)).
- Does my planning enable pupils to learn in a variety of ways?
- Are multisensory approaches embedded in my classroom practice?
- Am I providing opportunities for pupils to learn in areas of strength and to develop skills in other sensory modalities?

Management of group work

Effective group work is an essential component of teaching and learning. Teachers have a responsibility to plan for all pupils to develop the key skill of 'working with others'. Individual teaching has long been recognised as beneficial for pupils with SEN, although *earlier developments in the teaching of pupils with learning difficulties tended to concentrate on individual instruction to the exclusion of other approaches* (Marvin, 1998). Individual teaching is frequently a feature of IEPs where there is a focus upon individual learning. However, recognition of the benefits of working in groups and cooperative learning is also crucial to developing effective teaching and learning and promoting inclusive classrooms (e.g. Ainscow, 1995; Jenkins and O'Connor, 2003; Murphy et al., 2005). Indeed, for some pupils with SEN, aspects of 'working with others', through paired, group work and cooperative learning, are priority areas of learning that must be encouraged through carefully planned group work.

It is important that teachers acknowledge the significant difference between grouping and group work. Pupils are often located together around a table, all of them working at the same task. However, unless there is genuine collaboration in which the activities of the pupils are interdependent, this does not constitute group work. Simply locating pupils in close proximity (grouping) does not foster those skills of negotiation, collaboration and socialisation that are important to learning. Pupils need to engage actively with each other in order to learn from each other and develop the essential skills of cooperative learning.

Consideration of how to group pupils is at the heart of planning, and teachers will use diverse groupings depending upon the activity, learning objectives and so on. Ability, mixed ability, and friendship pairs and groups will all feature in the management of group work. The management of group work should, however, seek to go beyond simply thinking about how groups of pupils work alongside each other; it ought to promote 'cooperative learning' as a way for pupils to *work together to achieve team success in a manner that promotes the students' responsibility for their own learning as well as the learning of others* (Mercer and Mercer, 1998, p35). One approach that promotes active, cooperative learning is that of 'jigsawing'.

Jigsawing

The management of successful group work is challenging within inclusive contexts where pupils have a diverse range of learning needs (Gross, 1996). One approach worthy of consideration and reflection for developing successful group work is jigsawing. This approach to group work, developed during the 1970s, has been explored in mainstream schools (Aronson et al., 1978; Blaney et al., 1977), special school settings (Rose, 1991) and inclusive contexts (Howley and Arnold, 2003; Howley and Rose, 2005). Jigsawing involves careful planning for collaborative group work that facilitates 'positive interdependence' between participants (Johnson et al., 1990). Jigsawed planning fosters collaboration, with all participants having a vital role to play and therefore being encouraged to participate. This approach can be a successful strategy for planning group activities for pupils with diverse learning needs within mixed-ability groups. In addition, jigsawed planning can incorporate varied activities and tasks for developing 'multiple intelligences', with role observation, demonstration and rotation, as described by Kornhaber et al. (2004).

Jigsaw planning involves providing opportunities for pupils to work collaboratively in order for groups to be successful. Activities are divided into discrete parts, each of which is essential to the overall success of the task. Effective management of jigsawed planning leads to individual pupils and groups being interdependent, relying on everyone's participation to achieve success, either for the group or for the whole class. Discrete tasks may be allocated to individuals in a group to encourage group interdependence, or to groups within a class to achieve whole-class collaboration. Howley and Arnold

(2005) describe an activity designed as part of a school's 'book week' during which each class was involved in developing a book for another class. The example provided illustrates how one teacher planned for different groups to complete different tasks, one group writing the story, another group providing illustrations and another group designing and making pop-ups. Class success and achievement were dependent upon each group's participation. In addition, the teacher allocated different tasks to individuals within specific groups; for example, the illustrators were divided into pupils who drew pictures and other pupils who completed the art work by colouring and additional art work. Thus, interdependence was also created within the group (Figure 4.6).

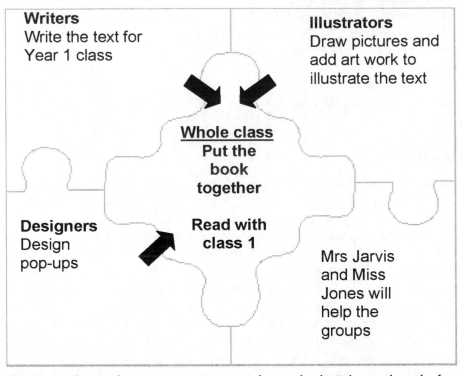

Figure 4.6 Jigsaw plan to promote group work. Boardmaker™ is a trademark of Mayer-Johnson LLC.

This approach has significant advantages in that the teacher can plan to provide multisensory activities and can allocate specific tasks to individuals according to their strengths, interests and learning styles. At the same time, pupils may benefit from observing others in their group who may be undertaking tasks that require different skills and strengths. Rotation of roles may provide opportunities for some pupils to develop skills across multiple intelligences, as in the example discussed by Kornhaber et al. (2004).

Jigsawing is a useful group management and planning strategy that may foster participation of pupils with SEN and promote peer support due to the interdependence created within the each group or the whole class. Pupils can be grouped in mixed abilities, encouraging more able pupils to support those who may have individual needs due to SEN. This type of group management promotes social skills and encourages and supports social interaction, often priority areas of learning for pupils with a range of SEN.

Management of group work and cooperative learning requires careful planning and evaluation. Murphy et al. (2005) provide useful recommendations for implementing cooperative approaches for pupils with learning difficulties, including the need to:

- create interdependence and individual accountability
- plan from the outset, defining, step-by step, all essential elements
- select suitable working partners
- teach cooperative learning social skills
- provide monitoring and reinforcement of use of social skills
- ensure sufficient time allocation to develop maturity of skills.

Jigsawing provides a structured strategy for teachers to develop and enhance opportunities for group work and cooperative learning, taking into account these recommendations.

Key questions and issues for reflection

- How do I plan group work and cooperative learning?
- How do I promote participation and foster interdependence?
- Are pupils, including those with SEN, being encouraged to work collaboratively?
- Am I providing opportunities for pupils to learn in areas of strength and to observe others in order to develop skills in other sensory modalities or to use multiple intelligences?
- What social skills are pupils learning through group work and cooperative learning?
- How will I monitor and evaluate the effectiveness of group work and cooperative learning?

Conclusion

Teaching and learning strategies in inclusive classrooms will be diverse and draw upon a range of approaches. Pupils with SEN may require specific strategies, individualised to support their learning. Managing individual learning requires teachers to reflect upon their own teaching styles and pupils' learning styles. However, effective teaching and learning, whilst recognising individual learning styles and cognitive profiles, should also seek to develop skills across multiple intelligences. Teachers in inclusive classrooms will respond to diverse individual needs by constantly monitoring and evaluating their own teaching, introducing varied teaching strategies and evaluating how pupils respond. Management of individual learning can seem daunting in the earlier stages of a teacher's career; nevertheless, as inclusive practitioners, teachers have a responsibility to manage individual needs within a whole-class context. Howley and Kime (2003) identify key principles that they suggest *underpin the successful management of individual learning of all pupils*, including the following recommendations:

- Specialised teaching strategies will be more successful, and of benefit to many pupils, if they are adapted for use within a class context, at the same time addressing the individual needs of specific pupils.
- Recognition of the learning needs of all pupils should form part of the inclusive classroom and school ethos to enable pupils to develop awareness, understanding and appreciation of individual differences.

This chapter has considered the importance of reflecting upon teaching and learning in order to develop awareness of teaching styles and learning styles. As Newton (2005) points out, *the key here is variety. No single method or approach works for everything* (p20). Pupils' differences in learning styles and differences in cognitive profiles inevitably demand diverse teaching strategies that can meet individual needs, but at the same time can be managed within a whole-class context. 'Specialist' strategies may be advocated for pupils with particular SEN, but the 'specialist' nature of these approaches should not deter inclusive teachers from considering their use in inclusive classrooms. Such strategies should not be exclusive; rather, we should strive to reflect upon the use of individualised, specialist approaches within the inclusive classroom context and the possible merits of introducing such approaches for the benefit of all pupils.

5   Creating inclusive classroom environments

Overview

This chapter will address the following issues:

- creating effective learning environments
- classroom structure and organisation: physical structure, access to resources, rules and routines
- classroom communication: alternative and augmentative communication, and communication aids.

Introduction

Inclusive classrooms promote the participation of all pupils, inclusion being a *process of increasing participation in ... mainstream social settings* (Booth et al., 1997). Within this theme of pupil participation, Florian (1998) discusses a range of conditions for promoting inclusive practice, including opportunities for pupil participation in decision making, positive attitudes, teacher knowledge about the learning abilities and difficulties of all pupils, skilled use of specific teaching methods and parent support of teachers (p22). Florian goes on to suggest that all conditions are essential to promoting inclusive education and that no single condition is sufficient. Acceptance of this diverse range of conditions necessitates close consideration of their components. One key component, and the focus of this chapter, is the need to appraise the classroom environment in order to assess its effectiveness in promoting the participation of all pupils.

The English National Curriculum indicates that schools and teachers should be *creating effective learning environments* (DfEE/QCA, 1999, p31) as part of developing inclusive practice, and statutory guidance for inclusive schooling (DfES, 2001) recognises the need to take 'reasonable steps' to promote inclusion. Consideration of the learning environment is therefore essential when developing, and reflecting upon, inclusive classrooms.

Certain features of classroom environments are recognised as pivotal to successful classroom management, including, for example, classroom layout and organisation, class rules and routines, and organisation of resources (Leggett, 2005; Newton, 2005). Features of the classroom environment have also been discussed in relation to particular individual needs arising from SEN. For example, Schopler et al. (1995) and Mesibov and Howley (2003) consider the importance of 'physical structure', one component of structured teaching, for pupils with ASD; classroom organisation, seating arrangements and grouping for pupils with learning difficulties are discussed by Farrell (1997); Waine and Kime (2005) describe organisation and location issues when assessing pupils with dyslexia; and Cockerill (2005) outlines the need to consider ergonomics in the classroom, focusing in his paper upon 'supportive seating' as a component of creating a 'supportive climate' in all classrooms, and advocating the need for specialist seating for some pupils with SEN. Access to resources is also a key feature of the classroom, with consideration given to individual needs such as shelf heights and ready availability of resources, including specialist equipment (Byers, 2001). Finally, another essential feature of the classroom environment is that of classroom communication. Alternative and augmentative communication systems will be integral to the effective inclusive classroom; for example, Carpenter and Morris (2001) indicate that visual communication systems can be of benefit for pupils with Down's syndrome, ASD and learning difficulties.

Whilst each of these examples relate to pupils with individual needs arising from particular disorders, the principles are neither unique nor exclusive to pupils identified with particular SEN. Features of the classroom environment should be considered in relation to all pupils, and many of the suggestions outlined for pupils with SEN will be relevant to all pupils. Teachers in inclusive classrooms will need to evaluate the effectiveness of their classroom environments both in relation to the needs of all pupils and through making adaptations and adjustments for individuals where needed. Careful appraisal of the classroom environment is integral to planning, as components of the environment will of course vary depending upon the lesson context.

The classroom environment will therefore either facilitate or impede participation and must be addressed if teachers are truly to include and engage pupils; failure to consider factors within the environment may at best result in some pupils being 'included' in body only and, at worst, result in classroom exclusions. This chapter explores two key aspects of a successful, inclusive classroom environment: classroom structure and organisation and classroom communication. Features of the classroom environment are considered, and ways of adapting the environment to promote participation and inclusion for all are illustrated. Classroom communication and the need to consider alternative and augmentative communication strategies are discussed with illustrative case studies. Key questions and issues are identified in order to encourage reflection of this important aspect of teaching, learning and inclusive practice.

Classroom structure and organisation

Some approaches, developed for pupils with varying SEN, emphasise the importance of considering the classroom environment. The layout of the classroom, positioning of furniture, seating arrangements, location of specific areas for specific activities, arrangements of displays and reduction of distraction are important features of the classroom that affect pupil participation and inclusion. Often teachers adopt particular layouts, perhaps ones that they have observed to be effective in the classrooms of other teachers. However, these may not always be the most effective, as the context of any classroom is ever-changing and depends upon pupil needs, abilities and personalities. By regularly reviewing classroom structure and organisational strategies, teachers may develop classroom environments that are more conducive to pupil participation. In addition to thinking generally about classroom organisation, it may be helpful to reflect upon strategies developed for pupils with specific needs in order to develop a more inclusive classroom environment.

Physical structure

One specific approach that addresses the learning environment is 'structured teaching', discussed in Chapter 4. The approach, developed to meet the particular needs of pupils with ASD, comprises key elements, three of which are illustrated in the previous chapter, and also a fourth element, that of 'physical structure' (Mesibov and Howley, 2003; Schopler et al., 1995). Physical structure relates closely to features of the classroom environment, and for pupils with ASD, consideration of the physical structure of the learning environment asks two key questions:

- Do pupils understand the purpose of space within this particular learning environment (e.g. classroom, hall, gymnasium, playground)?
- Are there potential distractions in the environment and how can these be minimised?

These questions are particularly pertinent to responding to the individual needs of pupils with ASD, who may be confused by the purposes of space and distracted by features of the environment due to sensory hypersensitivity. However, these needs are not exclusive to those with ASD, and consideration of these questions may well provide benefits for other pupils, such as those with ADHD or learning difficulties. Advocates of structured teaching recommend that in considering the physical structure of the classroom, teachers should do the following:

- Organise the classroom to ensure that pupils understand the purposes of space within the learning environment.
- Designate specific areas in the room for specific activities.
- Reduce potential distractions.

For pupils with ASD, or other SEN, assessment of need in this respect will be essential in order to adapt the environment. The following case study illustrates how the assessed needs of one pupil were met within an inclusive classroom.

Considering physical structure to meet individual needs

Tom has recently begun Year 1 at his local primary school. He has a diagnosis of autism and individual needs in the key areas of social interaction, communication and flexibility. Observations during Reception, and on entry to Year 1, reveal the following problems:

- aimless wandering round the classroom
- never in the right place at the right time
- difficulty in knowing where to sit (despite having an allocated seat at a group table) and anxiety when sitting with a group
- problems sitting on the carpet with the whole class
- high levels of distractibility especially in relation to visual distractions such as displays (When delivering the introduction to a literacy lesson, the teacher noticed that Tom did not listen, but was distracted by and absorbed in the displayed number line on the wall behind the teacher.)
- poor concentration and limited ability to stay on task when working in a group
- high levels of anxiety resulting in outbursts and tears.

These problems were considered to be priority learning areas and necessary preconditions to developing more effective teaching and learning strategies for Tom and his teacher. The class teacher and teaching assistant reviewed the organisation of the classroom and made the following adaptations in order to meet Tom's individual needs:

- reorganisation of furniture to make boundaries between specific areas clearer – e.g. bookcases were placed to mark the boundary between work tables and the whole-class teaching area on the carpet
- introduction of an independent 'workstation' for Tom to use at planned times during the day, this being placed in a corner of the room with a screen to reduce distractions from the rest of the class
- introduction of a carpet square for Tom to sit on during carpet time, this being initially placed on the periphery of the class to help Tom to build up tolerance to proximity to large numbers of children

- introduction of a name label that could be placed at any seating area designated by the teacher for Tom
- consideration of seating arrangements for Tom when working in a group; i.e. placing him in a position that did not face a window or display (to reduce visual distractions) and with a space between Tom and the adjacent peer
- reduction of visual distractions – e.g. covering the number line unless it is relevant to the lesson
- introduction of a 'quiet area' for Tom to withdraw to and learn self-calming strategies.

In the preceeding case study, the changes to the classroom structure and organisation are vital adaptations if Tom is to develop important skills such as listening, concentrating, staying on task and working alongside others. In this case study, the reorganisation of the classroom was considered in order to respond to Tom's individual needs, yet it subsequently proved to have benefits for other pupils. The teacher decided to use name labels to designate seating places for the whole class; these could be moved to change pupil groupings and proved to be an effective management strategy in that the teacher could ensure that pupils who disrupt or distract each other did not always sit together! Clear designation of specific areas, such as an independent workstation, enhanced the existing designation of areas for specific curriculum subjects, including a literacy centre. The workstation introduced for Tom could also be used by other pupils when appropriate, and the teacher subsequently introduced a second workstation so that she could plan for pupils to work individually in order to concentrate and stay on task. This benefited other pupils with SEN and also could be used by any other pupil who might, on occasion, for a range of reasons, need a quiet place to work. Labelling of specific areas, resources and so on was also improved, with written and symbol labels, for the benefit of all. Reduction of visual distractions for Tom also proved useful for others who were distractible, and the addition of a visual cue to remind Tom to 'listen' was used with the whole class (see below, under the heading, 'Classroom communication'). In addition, the quiet area provided opportunities to teach Tom to withdraw at times of overstimulation and to manage his outbursts. The provision of a catalogue for him to look through proved to be a useful self-calming strategy. This area was also used by the teacher for other pupils who might benefit from short periods of withdrawal to calm down or to reduce anxiety.

Further examples of how 'physical structure' can be considered in inclusive classrooms are illustrated by Mesibov and Howley (2003), who describe the use of independent workstations set up as an 'office' in a Key Stage 2 class (p35). The 'office' is used at planned times by pupils with varying SEN, with an office rota making the workspace available for all children at other times. Similarly, other features of physical structure can be used effectively in inclusive classrooms. A carpet square introduced for one pupil at whole-class teaching times can be introduced for any child who can not sit still; one Reception class teacher introduced the carpet square for the whole Reception class in assemblies because most of the children found it challenging to sit still in this context. Thus, the benefits of physical structure, essential in meeting the needs of those pupils with ASD, can be used for the benefit of many pupils in a class.

Access to resources

Access to resources is another essential component of the physical environment, and again pupils with individual needs require varied strategies for ensuring access. Byers (2001) reminds us that *decisions about the availability to pupils of resources and equipment can have a significant impact upon their development as independent learners* (p222). It may be helpful to put yourself in the shoes of individual pupils in order to consider access from their particular viewpoint. Pupils with mobility difficulties will need resources to be as easily accessible as they are for able-bodied pupils; this often requires a balance between ensuring that resources are accessible and encouraging independence. The teacher who relies upon a teaching assistant (TA) to provide resources and materials for a lesson for individual pupils may be ensuring access to resources, but may also be limiting the pupils' independence in relation to selecting appropriate materials for themselves. Specific organisational strategies, such as where to put finished work and where to put work that is unfinished, may be particularly useful for pupils who are disorganised. Pupils who become distracted or disorganised when out of their seat, or pupils with mobility difficulties, may benefit from the use of a resources basket provided at the group table for easy location of resources and to enable them to tidy resources independently. In addition, some pupils will need ready access to specific resources such as personal computers, tape recorders or communication aids; it is imperative that such resources be accessible at all times, as *integral parts of general classroom activity* (Byers, 2004). Other resource considerations include the use of displays, with careful thought needed in relation to where particular displays should be positioned for all pupils to be able to access the content. Often the solution for increasing independent access to resources is quite straightforward to achieve, yet this issue may be one that is overlooked; talking to pupils about their needs and involving the class in improving easy, independent access for all is important both for managing the inclusive classroom and for promoting positive participation and independence.

Rules and routines

In addition to evaluating the effectiveness of the structure of the learning environment, routines and rules are important features of the inclusive classroom. Children usually respond positively to routines that offer security and rules that clarify expectations. Establishing clear and positive routines and rules forms an integral part of any classroom organisation. Newton (2005, p44) provides an example of a teacher establishing a 'queuing routine' during a design and technology lesson that was then extended to become a general routine in any lesson when materials were to be distributed. Other common classroom routines include silence during registration to mark the beginning of the day and tidying the classroom to mark the end of the day. Newton (2005) reminds us that such routines should be *planned and practised until they become almost self-running* (p45). Similarly, the establishment of classroom rules is common classroom practice. Rules relating to expected behaviours are often explicit, especially in early years classrooms, as pupils are taught the social rules of the classroom such as raising their hands if they want to answer a question addressed to the class; such rules become embedded within everyday practice, although expectations may become more implicit during Key Stage 2. Children may be involved in generating and displaying the class rules, thus promoting ownership of the rules and encouraging appropriate behaviours.

The development of routines and rules is no different when considering the inclusion of pupils with SEN, although there may be individual needs and issues to be appraised. In addition to general class routines and rules, it may be helpful to consider specific strategies for pupils with SEN. Routines and rules that are devised in response to individual needs will often be useful to other pupils and may enhance the classroom practices already in place.

For example, the introduction of a 'first ..., then ...' routine, as in the structured teaching approach, can be essential for pupils with ASD or learning difficulties, who may be confused by sequences of activities – this routine indicates clearly that there is an expected order and clarifies the difference between activities that have to be completed and choice. Visual representation of these types of routines may enhance their meaning for some pupils (see the following section and Figure 5.1).

Classroom rules should be positive, indicating what to do rather than what not to do. Thus, the reframing of a rule such as 'don't call out' to 'remember, hand up' can be extremely helpful for pupils who have difficulty processing the 'negative' language components of an instruction, and this reframing also focuses upon desired behaviours rather than on the unacceptable. Such rules may also be presented visually to enhance meaning for some pupils (see the following section and Figure 5.2).

Children with SEN may require individualised routines and rules, in addition to those already in place. However, individualised strategies may be of benefit for other pupils and may enhance practice; for example, visual reminders relating to answering questions (i.e. remember, hand up) may initially be introduced in response to an individual need but may, in practice, serve as a useful reminder to all pupils, as illustrated by the example of 'David' in the video resource for supporting pupils with SEN in the literacy hour (DfEE, 2000).

Key questions and issues for reflection

- How effective is the organisation of the learning environment? Have I considered my classroom (or other context) layout and the purposes of space, seating, designation of specific areas, such as the need for a workstation or quiet area, and potential distractions?
- Can all pupils access required resources easily and independently?
- What are the established routines in my classroom? Do pupils know what the routines are? Do I need to consider any individual needs to develop more effective routines?
- Are pupils aware of the class rules? Are the rules framed in a positive way? Do I need to consider any individual needs to develop more effective rules?

Classroom communication

Effective communication is a vital element of any classroom, teaching and learning depending upon teachers' and pupils' communication skills. Reflecting upon and evaluating how you communicate with all pupils, and how you promote and enhance communication to respond to individual needs, will help you to improve classroom communication and consequently the quality of teaching and learning experiences. Some pupils with particular individual needs will face challenges in this area, such as pupils with speech and language difficulties, ASD, sensory impairments or learning difficulties. Teachers in inclusive classrooms must address communication within their classrooms in order to promote effective teaching and learning. This may involve thinking about using alternative and augmentative communication systems to enhance and support spoken language.

Alternative and augmentative communication

Alternative and augmentative communication systems should be integral to the inclusive classroom. Whilst spoken language, together with non-verbal signals, is the predominant mode, or system, of communication in many classrooms, some pupils with SEN will be excluded if this is the sole mechanism for communicating. Symbol communication has become common practice in special school settings, as schools use symbols for a variety of purposes, with particular benefits and application for teaching literacy (Abbott and Lucey, 2005). A range of symbols are being used in special schools, including Widgit Rebus, Makaton (signs and symbols) and picture communication systems (PCS), such schools often using a combination of systems (Abbott and Lucey, 2005). 'Specialist' communication systems also exist for pupils with specific needs, such as the picture exchange communication system (PECS) for pupils with ASD at early, preverbal stages of communication (Bondy and Frost, 1994). The use of alternative communication systems could, indeed, should, be extended to inclusive classrooms in mainstream schools; for example, Brower and Barber (2005) suggest using visual supports *when words are not enough*.

Effective use of alternative systems does not replace, but enhances teaching and learning. The use of objects, pictures, signs, symbols and written words, matched to individual needs, should be integral to classroom practice for supporting teaching and learning across all curriculum subjects and for clarifying expectations in the classroom. The following case studies illustrate the use of alternative communication systems in inclusive classrooms.[1]

Enhancing communication through objects

Billy is 4 years old and attends his local primary school, where he is included in a Reception class, and also spends time in a unit for pupils with SEN. Billy has a speech and language disorder and has limited understanding of spoken words but is beginning to recognise pictures as symbolic representations of activities or events. The inclusive Nursery setting had previously introduced objects of reference to inform Billy of the sequence of activities during the day. This has been continued in the unit, and pictures have now been attached to Billy's objects to aid his understanding of their symbolic significance. Billy can now independently follow his visual timetable. For Billy to be included in the Reception class, consistency in object/picture use is paramount, and he therefore uses the same system in this class to enable him to follow the sequence of activities. This system enhances the teacher's directions to the class about the 'order of the day'.

In addition, the teacher uses objects and pictures during lessons, such as objects/pictures in a story sack during a literacy lesson; these visual cues are essential for Billy, but are also useful for other pupils in the class. As Billy's vocabulary is extended, the TA prepares appropriate object/picture cues, under the direction of the speech and language therapist.

Enhancing communication through symbols

Pravin is in Year 1 of his local primary school. He has learning difficulties and while he understands routine spoken language, he has difficulty expressing himself through verbal language. Pravin recognises some high-frequency words.

After a class trip to a local museum, the class produce chronological accounts of their day. Pravin used 'writing with symbols' to complete sentences, prepared by the teaching assistant, in order to recount his day (Figure 5.1).

---

1 The website www.do2learn.com provides freely downloadable symbols, which may be useful for teachers who wish to try out symbol communication before purchasing software.

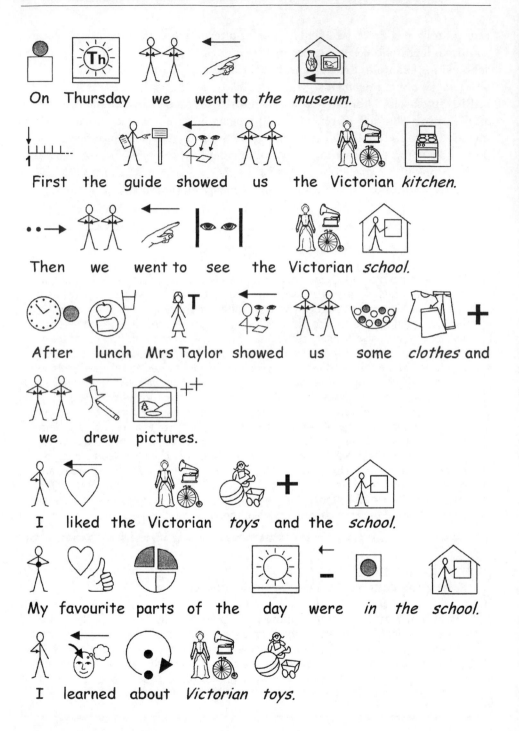

On Thursday we went to *the museum.*

First the guide showed us the Victorian *kitchen.*

Then we went to see the Victorian *school.*

After lunch Mrs Taylor showed us some *clothes* and

we drew pictures.

I liked the Victorian *toys* and the *school.*

My favourite parts of the day were *in the school.*

I learned about *Victorian toys.*

Figure 5.1 Communication enhanced with symbols. Widgit Rebus Symbols © Widgit Software, Tel: 01223 425558; www.widgit.com

Enhancing communication through written words

Tom is in Year 5 and has a diagnosis of Asperger's syndrome. His advanced expressive language and vocabulary masks his difficulties with comprehension of verbal language. Tom has poor short-term working memory, so, while he may appear to understand verbal directions during the introduction to a lesson, he is not able to recall the sequence during the main activities. However, Tom has the potential to excel in some areas of the curriculum, and his teacher is keen to extend him. Tom is identified as a visual learner; in particular, written words are more meaningful for him than spoken. In response, Tom is provided with written sequences of instructions to enable him to recall the sequence of directions given to the class. In this case, visual written words are used to enhance spoken language.

Tom's teacher extended this approach by providing written task cards for groups of pupils – visual reminders of the sequence of instructions enable pupils to focus upon task concepts, rather than spending time trying to recall what the teacher had said at the beginning of the lesson. Symbol/written instructions can facilitate access for non-independent readers.

In addition to enhancing verbal communication through concrete and visual means, it is also helpful to consider how visual systems might be incorporated into everyday classroom management. The need for rules and routines, described above, is essential to all classrooms; such rules and routines can be presented with additional visual cues and supports to ensure that all pupils understand their meaning (see, for example, Figures 5.2 and 5.3).

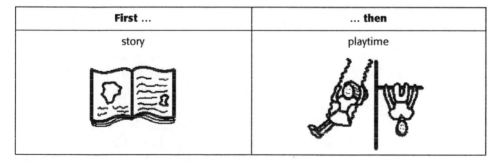

First ...	... then
story	playtime

Figure 5.2 Visual presentation of a 'first ..., then ...' routine for a pupil in Reception class.

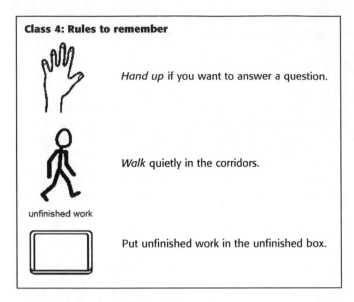

Figure 5.3 Visual representation of positive rules. Boardmaker™ is a trademark of Mayer-Johnson LLC.

Communication aids

The introduction of alternative and augmentative communication systems may, for some pupils, require specialist equipment and/or knowledge. A pupil who communicates by British Sign Language will need support from a specialist signer; however, learning basic key signs will improve the teacher's communication and interaction with that pupil. Equally important is the need to encourage all pupils to communicate with others who may have individual needs in this area; thus, for example, teaching the whole class some signs will enhance communication for all pupils in the class that includes a child with a hearing impairment. Similarly, some pupils benefit from, indeed require, specialist electronic communication systems, and teachers will need to be familiar with how these work. Wright et al. (2006) emphasise the importance of training for teachers to feel confident about using communication aids. Their research has shown that with appropriate assessment and training, the impact of communication aids in the classroom can be beneficial in a number of areas, including increased pupil involvement in class discussion, increased interaction in group work, increased confidence and reduced isolation (Wright et al., 2006). However, for communication aids of any type, it is essential that teachers are well trained in their use to ensure that these communication aids are exploited to their full potential. In addition, it is important to maintain consistency and to ensure that support is effective at all times. Specialist support must be followed through and may sometimes need alternative communication supports. The following case study illustrates the use of a communication book.

Wayne, a Year 3 pupil with significant hearing loss, receives support for some lessons from a communication support worker who is proficient in British Sign Language. Wayne's teacher, Elizabeth, has learned a few signs but is neither experienced nor qualified in the use of British Sign Language. When the communication support worker is not available, Elizabeth uses a communication book with Wayne. This contains pictures and symbols with which Wayne can construct simple sentences to make his needs known. Elizabeth incorporates many of these pictures and symbols into displays around the classroom and uses them in work that she prepares for Wayne. Wayne is gradually becoming more confident in picking up clues around the classroom to help his understanding and participation. His classmates have learned a few basic signs to help him to socialise and participate in lessons. With the additional support of the communication book, he is gaining the skills which enable him to participate in a hearing classroom.

Finally, in addition to considering alternative and augmentative communication systems and the use of specialist aids, you may also consider how to improve your own communication to pupils by considering the following:

- Be clear and concise when giving directions.
- Simplify language and limit vocabulary to key words for pupils who have difficulty with comprehension.
- Limit use of idioms and metaphorical language for pupils with social/communication difficulties (e.g. Asperger's syndrome).
- Break down tasks into steps and present instructions step by step for pupils with learning difficulties.
- Provide visual (picture/symbol/written word) topic vocabularies to pupils to refer to as you introduce new vocabulary.

Key questions and issues for reflection

- How effective is my communication in the classroom?
- Can I introduce alternative and augmentative communication systems to enhance meaning and understanding?
- Can I add visual cues to support classroom routines and rules?
- Am I familiar with communication aids used by individual pupils?
- Do I require further training to ensure best use of communication aids?
- Are pupils able to communicate with each other in a variety of ways?

Conclusion

There are many essential features of inclusive classrooms. Classroom structure, organisation, rules and routines, and access to resources form an essential component and, together with careful consideration of classroom communication, will enable teachers to reflect upon the key elements of providing an effective learning environment. Good teachers communicate effectively with pupils and with other adults in the class. They also recognise that there is much to be gained from listening to the views of the pupils in their care who have insights into those approaches and resources that can assist them to become more effective learners. As an inexperienced teacher, you will inevitably need time to gain the necessary confidence to develop your own teaching style and to address the diverse range of needs in your classroom. This chapter has described a set of principles that may assist you to become more confident in managing an inclusive classroom. However, it is important to recognise that the skills required to become effective in meeting the wide range of needs presented by pupils in today's primary classrooms will be achieved only through consistent practice built upon a determination to provide quality learning opportunities for every pupil.

6   Creating inclusive classroom teams

Overview

This chapter will address the following issues:

- The need for partnership
- Working effectively with support staff
- Partnership with other professionals
- Other adults in the classroom: parents, students and volunteers
- The role of peers.

Introduction

Teachers do not work in isolation but are involved in a range of partnerships in order to meet the needs of all pupils successfully. The *Every Child Matters* agenda emphasises a partnership approach to improve outcomes for children and families. Pupils with SEN are frequently involved with and supported by a range of partners in their learning and collaborative, and team partnerships are a crucial element of inclusive practice. The SEN code of practice (2001) and the government strategy for SEN (DfES, 2004b) both emphasise the importance of partnership in meeting the needs of pupils with SEN in mainstream schools.

As a teacher in an inclusive classroom, you will inevitably be required to work with others as part of a collaborative team in order to meet the needs of all pupils, including those with SEN. The inclusive classroom team is likely to comprise a number of partners, including the following:

- teaching assistants (TAs)
- other adults in the classroom, such as students and volunteers
- professionals from education, health and social care

- parents
- the pupil
- the pupil's peers.

As a teacher, you will be involved in a number of different ways with a variety of partners; your role will vary, depending upon the focus of the partnership, and may include the need to lead and direct a team, to work collaboratively with other professionals, to respond to advice and provide feedback to others, and to support pupils and parents or carers. This chapter focuses upon key issues in developing effective inclusive teamwork and provides examples to encourage you to reflect upon your own approaches to collaborative practice.

Working effectively with support staff

There is an increasing number of TAs and learning support assistants (LSAs) in schools in order to support diverse individual needs. The Warnock Report (DES, 1978) and the subsequent Education Act (DES, 1981) initiated integration into mainstream school for pupils with SEN, and it quickly became clear that for this to be successful, teachers would need support from other adults. The inclusion agenda was emphasised in a Green Paper in 1997 and again led to a significant rise in classroom support professionals. The focus upon 'raising standards' has also led to an increase in support staff, for example, in relation to supporting literacy and numeracy (DfES, 2002). Workforce remodelling (2003) and the Primary National Strategy (PNS)(2005) have helped to continue to acknowledge and develop the role of support staff, including the role of support assistants in relation to the inclusion of pupils with SEN.

The inclusion statement and principles identified in the National Curriculum (DfEE/QCA, 1999) emphasise the importance of ensuring access for pupils with SEN. The DfES suggest that *providing additional adult support for children or groups is a widely used access strategy* (2002), and research indicates that the majority of teachers see the role of support staff as essential for the successful inclusion of pupils with SEN in mainstream schools (e.g. Florian and Rouse, 2001; Rose and Coles, 2002). However, the same researchers suggest that the roles of these critical professional colleagues have not always been well defined. The many varying titles of support staff reflect their diverse roles, including TA, higher-level teaching assistant (HLTA), LSA, classroom assistant, nursery nurse (NNEB), additional literacy and/or mathematics support assistant, bilingual support assistant, and ancillary support assistant. Indeed, you may find yourself responsible for directing the work of a number of support staff, whose roles may vary. Different types of support staff are involved in different classrooms, and this inevitably means that the nature of the partnership between teachers and support assistants varies from one setting to another.

However, the aims of support are more clearly defined with an increased move toward developing a flexible teacher/pupil support model, in which the assistant supports both the pupils and the teacher. The DfEE (2000) Good Practice Guide identifies the nature of support within four strands: support for the *pupil*, support for the *teacher*, support for the *curriculum* and support for the *school*. Within this model, there will inevitably be diversity in relation to practice, depending upon school ethos, classroom practice and individual needs. In addition, the Centre for Educational Needs (1999) suggests that effective practice should:

- foster the *participation* of pupils in the social and academic processes of the school
- seek to enable pupils to become more *independent learners*
- help to *raise standards.*

In an attempt to clarify the role of support staff, Garner and Davies (2001) identify the following features as characteristic of the role of the TA:

- helping teachers with planning
- preparation and differentiation of curriculum materials
- organisation to enable differentiation
- working with individuals, groups and the whole class
- supporting IEPs
- providing additional explanations
- keeping children on task
- managing behaviour
- reviewing pupil progress with the teacher
- staff development and professional development
- liaising with parents/carers.

The Primary National Strategy also provides useful guidance in relation to the management of TAs to improve standards in literacy and mathematics (DfES, 2003c); in particular, the role of the TA in relation to joint planning and progress reviewing with the teacher should include the following components:

- termly/half-termly reviews
- in-service training
- timetabled weekly meetings
- ongoing informal feedback
- shared booklet or recorded memos
- computer based records.

Moreover, Rose (2000) suggests that *the effective use of Teaching Assistants is a key factor in developing moves towards greater inclusion....* and identifies three principles for providing effective support:

- Benefits of support are for all pupils, not just those with SEN.
- Collaboration between teachers and LSA is essential at all stages of planning and evaluation of lessons.

- Allocating LSA to named teachers rather than pupils may enhance effective collaborative practices.

The diverse roles of support staff present challenges in terms of managing support effectively, but, as Bradley and Roaf suggest, *beginning teachers need to develop the pattern of support which works for them and cultivate the opportunities to talk over difficulties with experienced staff who have time to lend a listening ear* (Bradley and Roaf, 2000, cited in Garner and Davies, 2001). It is your responsibility, probably with support from the SENCO, to manage and monitor the work of support assistants. It is essential therefore that you are able to build effective teams and develop successful ways of teamwork, for, as Bartholomew and Bruce (1993) suggest, *when adults work together and use their energy in an orchestrated way on behalf of the child, then quality and excellent progress are seen.*

The following case studies provide examples of teachers and support staff working as a team in order to develop effective inclusive practice, focusing upon planning, clear role definition and communication.

Sharing planning

Mrs Taylor is a Year 6 teacher in an inclusive primary school that also has a specialist unit for pupils with particular individual needs. The Year 6 class includes a number of pupils with varying individual needs. In addition, one pupil in the class spends half of his time in the class and half in the unit. Mrs Taylor has a TA for 75% of the week and additional support from the unit to provide support for an individual pupil.

The school plan on a rolling 2-year cycle, allowing for joint planning for Years 5 and 6. Team planning meetings take place on a regular basis and include all teachers and TAs of Years 5 and 6. TAs contribute to planning and in particular may be involved in differentiating resources and strategies for pupils with SEN. However, the teacher responsible for the unit is not always able to attend all planning meetings, and the LSA who joins Mrs Taylor's class is not in school during planning meetings.

In line with school policy, all medium-term planning is available on a computerised system at least half a term in advance. In addition, Mrs Taylor's daily lesson plans are available on the same system, allowing access to planning for all teachers, including the teacher in the unit, and all support staff. This ensures that all staff are familiar with planning and their roles within each lesson. This is essential for effective teamwork during each lesson. In addition, with access to planning, the unit staff can prepare individual pupils in advance for specific lessons, such as introducing new topic vocabulary prior to a lesson. They can also liaise with class teachers and support staff in order to differentiate effectively for individual pupils.

This case study illustrates how one school makes planning accessible to all staff; in this case, all planning is computerised. You may need to think about developing ways of sharing your planning with support staff, particularly if they are not available to be included in planning meetings. Lesson plans should be available in advance so that support staff are clear about your expectations and their role in each lesson. Teachers who involve and share planning with support staff will experience a number of benefits that will enhance inclusive practice; for example, a support assistant may have more in-depth knowledge about an individual pupil and may be able to differentiate resources and/or teaching strategies to promote curriculum access. Effective teamwork requires you to involve support staff in your planning. Together with support staff, you will develop your own ways of sharing planning with benefits for you, for the support assistant and for pupils.

Role definition

Jamie attends a local primary school where he is fully included in a Year 1 class. Jamie has a statement of SEN with a number of identified individual needs, including learning difficulties, lack of independence and poor concentration. Jamie has an LSA who provides support during whole-class teaching, group work and one-to-one teaching sessions across the curriculum.

After a review of Jamie's progress, an IEP target was set to develop his ability to complete two tasks independently. Jamie's teacher developed appropriate tasks relating to literacy and numeracy and planned for Jamie to work independently on two tasks on a daily basis. The SENCO arranged to observe Jamie to monitor his progress toward this target. Observations showed that whilst Jamie worked on the tasks provided, the LSA sat beside him and discussed what he was doing as he worked on each activity. The SENCO felt that this reduced Jamie's opportunities to work independently and asked the LSA why she sat next to him if the target was independent completion of the tasks. The LSA replied, 'If I do not sit with him, the teacher will think I am doing nothing.'

The lack of role definition resulted in an LSA being unclear of her role whilst the pupil she supports should be working independently. The SENCO discussed this with the teacher and LSA and suggested that the LSA could be used more effectively by allocating her a specific role while Jamie worked independently. It was agreed that the LSA could work with a group of children, at the same time keeping an eye on Jamie to ensure he stays on-task. This strategy would mean that other pupils would benefit from adult support whilst Jamie developed his independence.

This case study illustrates the importance of ensuring that support staff have clear roles and are not left 'guessing' what you would like them to do. Support staff can be involved in supporting pupils in diverse ways, and it is up to you, as the teacher, to discuss the most effective support roles with support staff.

These roles will vary according to the context and needs of pupils. Support staff may be involved in one-to-one support, group support and encouraging independence. In addition, it is important to define expectations of support roles during whole-class teaching. This is frequently a time when support staff are not fully utilised and may feel that they are 'guessing' what the teacher's expectations are. Roles should be made clear, and you should ensure this is also the case during whole-class teaching; rather than leaving the support assistant feeling like a 'spare part', allocate specific roles such as monitoring individual behaviours, encouraging individuals to participate or observing particular pupils. This will clarify and enhance the role of support assistant and is important in developing more effective teamwork.

Communication

Mr Davies is a newly qualified teacher (NQT) of Year 3 pupils in a mainstream primary school. Mrs Jones is a support assistant in this class; she is paid to arrive at school at 9.a.m. and she leaves at 12 noon. Whilst Mr Davies ensures that his planning is made available to Mrs Jones in advance and her role is clearly defined at each stage of the lesson, he feels that he has no time to discuss issues relating to progress of the pupils that Mrs Jones has been working with.

The school's SENCO is involved in allocating and monitoring the work of support staff. Mr Davies therefore approached the SENCO to ask for advice about how he could improve communication with his support assistant in order for her to provide feedback relating to pupil progress, achievement, any misconceptions or problems with particular tasks and pupil behaviour. Time constraints negate face-to-face discussion, but Mr Davies felt that he needed this feedback in order to inform his assessment and future planning. The SENCO suggested introducing a 'communication book' in which the support assistant could note any relevant information for Mr Davies. In addition, this book could also be used for Mr Davies to inform Mrs Jones of any last-minute changes to planning or for other issues that might arise if, for example, he requires her to observe a particular pupil during a lesson.

It is important for you to develop effective communication with support staff. Regular face-to-face meetings are highly desirable, but not always realistic. In this case, you will need to seek diverse ways of developing good communication in relation to sharing planning and to ensuring that you have necessary feedback from support assistants. Successful communication enhances effective teamwork, ensures that the role of support assistants is clearly defined and, most importantly, ensures that support assistants know that you value their role. Of course, you will through experience, find your own ways of leading and working effectively with the classroom team. Cremin et al. (2003) identify various models for teacher/support staff teamwork, including 'room management', in which adults have different responsibilities for different tasks within the classroom, and 'zoning', in which different adults concentrate on different parts of the classroom. You will most likely use a combination of approaches, but your main focus should be upon developing what Cremin et al. (2003) refer to as 'reflective teamworking' with support assistants.

Working collaboratively with support assistants will require you to:

- ensure the support assistants are aware of their role and responsibilities
- ensure that assistants are aware of school procedures and policies
- establish 'ground rules' such as methods of discipline in your classroom and how this 'fits' with the school's policy
- establish good communication
- establish regular meeting times to discuss organisation of class, day and week, planning and progress and problems; set up an alternative means of communication if regular meeting times are not possible
- ensure that the assistant is aware of the learning implications of the pupil's special need as appropriate
- make clear and realistic requests
- provide encouragement and feedback about the assistant's work.

Key questions and issues for reflection

- Is my support assistant clear about his or her role at all times?
- How do I involve my support assistant in my planning?
- How do I communicate with my support assistant to inform assessment and future planning?

Partnership with other professionals

In addition to working with support assistants, you will inevitably be required to work in partnership with professionals from other disciplines. Pupils with SEN may require support from other services, and fundamental to any effective intervention or approach will be consistency of approach and 'joined-up' teamwork among professionals. The *Every Child Matters* agenda emphasises the importance of multiagency working, indicating benefits in relation to outcomes for children and families and for staff and services. The SEN code of practice (2001) devotes a chapter to 'working in partnership with other agencies', identifying some key principles of interagency working for children with SEN. It states that:

> Meeting the special educational needs of individual children requires flexible working on the part of statutory agencies. They need to communicate and agree policies and protocols that ensure that there is a 'seamless' service. (p135)

Research indicates many benefits of collaborative partnerships; for example, Wright et al. (2006) indicate the importance of multidisciplinary assessment in developing effective use of communication aids, Howley et al. (2001) discuss partnership between an autism family support service and primary school-teachers, and Lacey (2001) describes how a shared culture of understanding of professional roles and how these can become more complementary can be achieved through developing structured partnerships between teachers and therapists.

The SEN code of practice (2001) states that provision should be *based on a shared perspective and should build wherever possible on mutual understanding and agreement* (p135). In practice, this means that you will need to work directly with professionals from other services in order best to meet individual needs. As a teacher in an inclusive primary school, you will be required to work with other professionals, including, for example, educational psychologists, speech and language therapists, physiotherapists, occupational therapists, advisory support services, and social care and health professionals. Some pupils with SEN will be involved with a range of services, and you will need to be able to liaise and work in partnership with all involved with the pupils and their family. This will require good communication and listening skills and confidence to share your own ideas and practice with others. The following case study illustrates partnership working with other professionals.

Working with a behaviour support service

Billy is 9 years old and attends his local primary school. He has ADHD and presents social, emotional and behavioural difficulties. Billy finds it difficult to stay on task and to complete activities, is disruptive in class and has frequent emotional outbursts. Billy's needs are met through school action plus and his class teacher, Mrs Bates, is working with the behaviour support service in order to meet his needs in the classroom.

Initially, an advisory teacher from the behaviour support service met with Billy's teacher, the SENCO and Billy's parents to discuss his needs at school and at home. Billy was observed in the classroom by the advisory teacher, who also discussed his needs, strengths, weaknesses and interests with him. Mrs Bates discussed the challenges Billy posed in the classroom and openly shared her practices and strategies with the advisory teacher, including successful and unsuccessful approaches to meeting Billy's needs. Following these discussions and observations, the advisory teacher made a number of recommendations and allocated a behaviour-support assistant from the behaviour-support team to provide regular input to assist with implementing specific strategies for managing Billy's behaviour in class.

Mrs Bates met with the behaviour-support assistant and the class LSA to discuss the approaches to be introduced, to identify how and when these approaches could be implemented across the curriculum, and to ensure that the class LSA was familiar with the approaches. A range of approaches were introduced, including:

- teaching Billy an organisational system to encourage him to complete one task independently each morning and afternoon
- introduction of visual cue cards to remind Billy of expected behaviour
- introduction of a self-monitoring, rewards and responsibilities system to support appropriate behaviour and to raise self-esteem
- establishing a regular one-to-one chat time with the LSA.

The behaviour-support assistant was given access to the teacher's planning in order to identify clear opportunities for implementing the approaches, and a system was set up for the LSA to monitor Billy's progress.

As Billy began to respond, a follow-up meeting with Mrs Bates, the SENCO, the teacher and their assistant from the behaviour-support team, and Billy's parents was set up in order to share practice and ideas for Billy's parents to try at home in order to develop consistency between school and home. Billy was also included in part of the meeting in order to seek his views.

This case study illustrates the need for, and importance of, collaborative working in order to meet one pupil's individual needs. As a teacher, you will need to be able to work effectively with other professionals in order to meet diverse needs. This will require a number of professional qualities:

- good communication and listening skills – you will need to be able to listen to and respond to the advice of other professionals
- confidence to share your ideas and practices with other professionals
- the ability to develop open, trusting relationships with others in order to work toward a shared agenda.

Key questions and issues for reflection

- Am I fully aware of the roles of other professionals involved with pupils in my class? If not, how could I find out?
- How effective are my communication and listening skills? If I do not know, how could I find out?
- Do I feel confident about sharing my ideas and practices with others? If not, what could I do about this?

Other adults in the classroom

In addition to managing and working in partnership with support assistants and collaborating with other professionals, you may also find that you have other adults to manage in the classroom. Parents and volunteers can be a useful additional resource when carefully managed and valued in the inclusive classroom. Bastiani (1989) suggests that parents and volunteers may volunteer to help in schools for three main reasons:

- to help their own children
- to help the school
- to meet their own needs.

Whatever the reason for volunteering, additional adult support can be of great value, but it requires confidence and good communication skills to develop a good working relationship. Teachers' fears about involving other adults in the classroom may include concerns about issues relating to unreliability, over enthusiasm, breaches of confidentiality, children showing off, complaints from other parents, people favouring their own children, and criticism by teachers and other staff. Management of other adults in the classroom requires high levels of professionalism, and in order to develop useful partnerships with parents and volunteers, the following issues need to be considered by the school and the class teacher:

- Senior management support: Does the senior management provide support and guidelines for managing other adults?
- Key staff responsible for parents and volunteers: Is there a key member of staff who is responsible for the overall management of parents and volunteers?
- Guidelines for parents and volunteers: Are there clear guidelines from the school for parents and volunteers? Do you provide clear guidelines for parent helpers and volunteers in your classroom?
- Communication strategies: How do you communicate with parent helpers and volunteers? How do they know what you want them to do? Do they know what the learning objectives are? Are they involved in giving you feedback?
- Skills: Have you considered the skills that parent helpers and volunteers can offer?
- Classroom management: Are parent helpers and volunteers familiar with class behaviour management and discipline procedures? Are they familiar with classroom organisation, rules and routines?
- Respect: Are all adults in the classroom treated with equal respect?

The following case study is illustrative of how some of these key issues and provides an example of good practice.

Involving other adults in the classroom

Mr Howard teaches a Year 3 class that includes pupils with a range of individual needs. In particular, some children have been identified as requiring additional support to develop their reading. The school has a clear policy regarding parent helpers and volunteers, and one member of staff on the senior management team (in this case, the deputy head) is responsible for the overall management of additional adults who volunteer. After a meeting with potential volunteers, the deputy head allocated a parent helper to Mr Howard's class for one morning per week to listen to individual readers. The helper allocated had expressed an interest in reading and also helped in the school library.

Mr Howard met with the parent helper, Mrs Smart, and discussed her role in listening to individual readers. Class rules were shared with Mrs Smart and clear guidelines were provided about classroom discipline and expectations. A group of eight children were identified by the teacher as pupils who would benefit from additional one-to-one reading. Mrs Smart was provided with learning objectives for each pupil, together with information about reading strategies that she should encourage for each pupil. She was also shown how to use the pupil reading record in order to record pupil progress and to provide feedback for the teacher. It was agreed that Mr Howard would provide a list of which pupils he would like to read to Mrs Smart during each visit so that she would not need to interrupt teaching to ask for directions.

This system was successful, and Mr Howard then discussed extending Mrs Smart's role to include a small group for guided reading. In addition to previous information provided for Mrs Smart, the teacher's literacy lesson plan was accessible to her, and further information was provided relating to learning objectives and strategies for her group. A record proforma was also provided for Mrs Smart to record pupil progress.

In this case, it is clear that the parent helper's role was clearly defined and valued, and a partnership approach ensured the best use of her time spent with individual pupils. Her contribution provided increased opportunities for individuals to receive support for their reading. This partnership approach is the key to managing other adults in the classroom for the benefit of pupils and teachers.

Key questions and issues for reflection

- How do I involve parent helpers and volunteers?
- How do I indicate the volunteer's role in your planning?
- How do they know what to do?
- How do I communicate with parent helpers and volunteers following the lesson?
- What do I do if the volunteer I am expecting does not turn up?

The role of peers

Inclusive classroom teams are likely to involve support assistants, other professionals, and helpers and volunteers. In addition, there is a further group who are key elements of this team, the peer group. Research demonstrates the importance of involving peers in supporting pupils with SEN, with benefits for individual pupils with SEN and for the peer group providing support.

Whitaker (2004) describes the role of mainstream 'peer tutors' as buddies in developing shared play and communication with pupils with severe autism in a unit attached to a mainstream school. 'Circles of friends' have been shown to have benefits for both the pupils with SEN and the members of the circle (e.g. Newton et al., 1996; Whitaker et al., 1998). Benefits for circle members included the development of empathy, problem-solving skills, listening skills, an ability to identify and express feelings, understanding of links between behaviour and feelings, increased awareness of the power to change, enhanced self-esteem, improved group participation and individual benefits. Whitaker et al. (1998) identified the benefits for pupils with SEN (in this research, ASD) as improved social integration, increased peer contact, reduced anxiety and improved behaviour. The role of peers and the use of 'inclusive' rewards that reward the class for their support, rather than merely the individual pupil with SEN, are described by Howley and Arnold (2005). Their example describes the role of a circle of friends and the peer group in encouraging appropriate social behaviour at playtimes, with an individual reward (marbles) for the pupil with SEN; accumulation of marbles for the individual resulted in extra 'golden time' for the class, thus encouraging peers to support the appropriate social behaviour expected of the individual pupil.

Therefore, it is clearly important not to overlook the role of peers; indeed, valuing their role as part of the inclusive classroom team may result in benefits for all involved. The responses of peers can be very important to individual pupils with SEN and may influence their behaviour and/or learning, both positively and negatively. As a teacher in an inclusive classroom, it is essential to consider the role of the peer group in supporting pupils with SEN through the use of a buddy approach, circles of friends and learning mentors.

Involving peers as buddies

Lena is in a Year 3 class in her local primary school. She arrived at the school from Russia at the end of Year 2. Lena speaks a little English and has been identified as having specific learning difficulties, particularly in literacy. Her mother expressed concern to the teacher, Mrs Hughes, about Lena's lack of friends and her low self-esteem, especially in relation to reading. Conversations with Lena revealed that she felt lonely at school, especially at playtime.

Mrs Hughes discussed Lena's needs with the SENCO, who suggested setting up a buddy system to help Lena to develop her relationships with peers. Lena agreed with this idea and said she would like a friendship buddy at playtime. Coinciding with this, the school had recently completed staff development in developing friendship buddies for whole-school playtimes, and pupils in Year 5 were being trained to take on this role. Lena's teacher devoted circle time to exploring this new initiative with the class. It was explained that while Year 5 pupils would be taking on the role of playtime buddies, it might be a good idea to introduce a buddy system for the class.

As a result, four pupils in the class were identified as being suitable potential buddies for Lena, and all four agreed they would be happy to take on the role. A meeting with these pupils, Lena and the TA resulted in the drawing up of a buddy rota for playtime, and Lena shared with the group her interests and likes. Consequently, Lena had a playtime buddy from her class to interact with each playtime. This led to her gradually becoming involved with wider circles of friendship groups as each buddy included Lena in activities with their friends. By the end of term, Lena was more fully included at playtime.

In addition, Lena was allocated a reading buddy from a Year 6 class for shared reading to provide her with extra opportunities for developing her reading. In turn, as she grew in confidence, she became reading buddy to a pupil in Year 1.

The preceeding case study illustrates the importance and value of involving peers as part of the inclusive classroom team. Lena's social needs were met more successfully by involving her peer group, and the introduction of a reading buddy helped to build her confidence. Benefits of involving peers in this way are clear for the individual pupil, but this involvement also has benefits for peers, enhancing their self-esteem, developing responsibility and empathy.

Learning mentors

Learning mentors have become a common feature of many schools, particularly those working within an 'extended schools' culture and attempting to develop as a community learning hub. In schools where learning mentors operate, they often act as critical friends to pupils who are deemed to be at risk or who may have a poor record of attendance or exclusion. Learning mentors are often perceived by pupils as being distinctly different from teachers or other staff and are regarded as someone to whom they can speak with confidence more as a friend than a person in a position of authority. The majority of teachers working in primary schools have very limited experience of working with learning mentors. If you are fortunate enough to find yourself in a school where they are being used, you are not likely to be much less familiar with their purpose than others in the school. It is important to remember that their function is one of offering direct support to pupils in difficulty and that they do not work in the same ways as other adults in the school. It is important that you seek advice from the head teacher with regard to the expectations of teachers in relation to working with learning mentors, who can often play a major role in ensuring that pupils are better equipped to participate in class. The following case study illustrates the role of a learning mentor.

Working with a learning mentor

Clive is a Year 6 pupil who has had a number of difficulties in school. He is regarded by most staff as a 'behaviour problem' and is often in trouble in school. Over the past two terms, his attendance record has been poor and he is often argumentative when he first arrives in the morning. For the past few weeks, Clive has been working with a learning mentor called Nick, who has made contact with Clive's parents and discussed how Clive feels about school with them and him. The parents both express a lack of confidence in visiting the school, having had poor experiences during their own school years and feeling that teachers are not easy to communicate with. Nick agrees a plan of action with Clive and his parents. Each morning he meets Clive at the school gate when his mother delivers him to school. He takes Clive in to school and spends the first 20 minutes of the day talking to him about the things which Clive chooses to discuss. After this, he takes Clive to the first lesson of the day and stays with him until he is settled in class. Each lunchtime and at the end of the day, Clive goes to see Nick to talk in general about how things are going. Nick does not report conversations with Clive to his teacher unless Clive asks him to act as an intermediary. However, Clive's teacher has noted that since beginning this intervention Clive appears more settled and cooperative in class. He has also maintained 100% attendance over recent weeks.

Key questions and issues for reflection

- How do I involve peers to support pupils with SEN? Can I find ways to develop peer support?
- What are the benefits of involving peers for pupils in my class who have SEN? What are the benefits for the peer group?
- How do I reward individual pupils and could I develop more inclusive rewards to encourage peer support?

Conclusion

Successful inclusive classrooms are those in which a collaborative, partnership approach is valued. As a teacher in an inclusive classroom, you will find it invaluable to invest time in building effective teams, with a shared agenda and shared goals for meeting individual needs. This may seem daunting at first, but as you gain experience and confidence, you will find your own ways of developing your role within a team approach. As you develop professional skills in this area, the following will be helpful:

- Discuss teamwork and collaboration with experienced colleagues, who will be able to demonstrate practices that they have found most effective.

- Consult the member of staff responsible for the management of support assistants in order to reflect upon and develop effective classroom teamwork.
- Seek advice from the SENCO in order to develop experience of working in partnership with other professionals.
- Discuss your ideas for involving peers with experienced colleagues.

Finally, do not forget that pupils with SEN are also part of the team; find out their views and value their contribution as part of the inclusive classroom team. Chapter 7 is devoted to 'learning from pupils'. Likewise, parents and carers are critical members of the team, and effective working in partnership with parents is essential to developing a team approach. Collaborating with parents and carers demands high-level professional skills; Chapter 8 looks beyond school and considers issues relating to developing partnerships with parents, carers and families.

7   Learning from pupils

Overview

This chapter will address the following issues:

- the importance of listening to the views of pupils
- recognising the skills required for pupil participation in self-assessment
- providing support to pupils in self-assessment
- involvement in target setting
- involvement in formal meetings and reviews.

Introduction

The teacher and pupil relationship is clearly critical in establishing routes to effective teaching. Your authority in the classroom is central to the maintenance of order, and the tone adopted by you will influence the ways in which pupils respond and the climate for learning. In the past, the role of the teacher was seen largely as one of a purveyor of knowledge, charged with the responsibility to educate pupils through the provision of information and the instilling of discipline. This didactic approach emphasised the authority of the teacher but often failed to acknowledge the importance of the learner as an autonomous individual capable of reasoning and learning through more enquiry-based approaches. There are, of course, times when didacticism is fully justified in order to convey new information or provide direct instruction to pupils. However, as our understanding of learning develops, it becomes increasingly apparent that pupils need to be provided with independent learning skills, including the ability to interrogate their own understanding, question the teacher and gain confidence in experimenting with new ideas and concepts. Vygotskian theory, and particularly that associated with the zone of proximal development (Vygotsky, 1982), informs us of the importance of guiding pupils to gain confidence through supported learning, and then to instil in them the conviction to challenge their own understanding in order to become autonomous learners. Vygotsky describes the zone of proximal development (ZPD) as the distance between what pupils already understand, and what they can do when supported by an adult. This theory suggests that your ability to interpret the current level of a pupil's learning is critical, as is the confidence of the pupil in recognising that, whilst the support which you provide is important, learning is most successfully achieved when a task can be performed independently. Autonomous learning can be achieved only when pupils are provided with opportunities to gain the confidence to express their own understanding of the learning situation and enter into a dialogue with you as the teacher about their own learning needs.

The learning of pupils described as having SEN is often characterised by dependency and an inordinate need for personal support. Teachers, when asked about the conditions required to include pupils with SEN in their classrooms, often cite the need for additional classroom support as a priority (Farrell and Balshaw, 2002; Giangreco, 1997). However, it has become increasingly apparent that ill considered use of TAs or other adult support, far from encouraging pupils to develop effective learning skills, can create dependency and inhibit such development (Cremin et al., 2003; Rose, 2001). Pupils who have their own allocated TA may well behave better in class and remain 'on task', but their opportunities to perform independently and therefore become more effective autonomous learners may be restricted. All pupils need time and space to learn through experimentation, to make mistakes and to learn to rectify these through problem solving. Adult intervention can at times inhibit problem-solving activity through intervention, that aims to provide errorless learning. Such a construct is unhelpful, as it creates an artificial learning situation in which pupils fail to take advantage of learning through personal enquiry and have few chances to consider alternative approaches to problems, and they have confidence in addressing tasks only when supported. Whilst all pupils need support in acquiring new skills and understanding, it is only through use and rehearsal of this new learning that they will gain the confidence to become effective learners. You will therefore need to encourage autonomy, to enable pupils to make choices and decisions and to assess their own performance in a classroom environment where they feel secure and assured that making mistakes or exhibiting less than perfect understanding is an accepted part of the learning process.

Pupil autonomy is not about teachers relinquishing control. It is much more about recognising that, through listening to pupils and encouraging them to discuss their own learning needs, you can become more effective in planning for, delivering and assessing learning. From a very young age, pupils are capable of expressing their opinions and making judgements about their own learning. Nutbrown (1996) emphasises that children learn lessons about human interaction when they are very young. This includes learning to communicate their ideas in an acceptable manner, to express their needs, and to respect the opinions of others. However, these skills are learned only when opportunities are provided for pupils to express themselves in a climate which demonstrates respect and encourages self-confidence. Griffiths and Davis (1995) have demonstrated that, when encouraged, even the youngest pupils can make informed judgements about their own academic performance and learning needs. They emphasise that teachers need to create classrooms in which pupils are supported in making evaluations of their own learning by adults in a climate of mutual understanding and respect. Effective teachers are acutely aware of the learning strengths and needs of the individual pupils in their classes. Such awareness enables them to plan and differentiate their lessons, to ensure that pupils are able to make progress from their current levels of learning, and to assess accurately the progress which they make. You can make this task considerably easier through the involvement of pupils who are encouraged to reflect upon and express their own learning achievements, needs and, in some cases, anxieties.

It may be assumed that pupils described as having SEN will not have the ability to make informed judgements about their own learning needs. Labelling pupils as having a learning difficulty may have the effect of lowering teacher expectations of their ability in this regard. Yet, there is evidence to suggest that pupils with the most complex learning needs, given appropriate support, can make accurate assessments of their own learning and can comment on those teaching approaches which either enhance or obstruct their progress (Fletcher, 2001). In his research, Fletcher emphasises that pupil abilities in making judgements about their own learning will be improved only if teachers provide both the opportunities and the structure to support such improvements. Making decisions or choices and being able to evaluate personal performance depend upon the acquisition of skills, knowledge and understanding, which must be taught. Teachers who work with reception classes are acutely aware of the fact that some pupils enter school having learned the fundamental social skills which enable them to share resources, take turns, make informed choices and express their ideas in an acceptable manner. Others, they report, come to school without having acquired any of these social necessities, and often it is these pupils who have greatest difficulties in adjusting to the social order of the classroom. The acquisition of these social skills is an essential component of becoming an effective learner. It is important to recognise that such skills are not simply acquired but have to be learned. Whilst, for some pupils, this learning takes place in the home and is modelled by parents, other adults or siblings, this will not be the case for some, and therefore teachers must be prepared to ensure that such skills are taught. Some pupils with learning difficulties may take longer to gain these social skills because of poor understanding. However, teaching pupils how to adjust their social behaviours to the expectations of the classroom will make both the management of the individual pupil by yourself and the ability of the pupil to participate in learning much easier. It will also prepare pupils to be able to make more informed judgements about their own learning needs and enable them to focus upon the expectations which you have of them.

Pupil involvement in assessment

Most of us learn more effectively when we have a clear view of what it is we need to learn, where we are relative to achieving this learning, and the actions which we are to take in making progress toward our learning goals. This is as true of pupils in primary classrooms as it is of ourselves as well-established and successful learners. The SEN code of practice (2001) recognises that

> Children and young people with special educational needs have a unique knowledge of their own needs and circumstances and their own views about what sort of help they would like to help them make the most of their education. (DfES, 2001a, para. 3:2, p27)

Teachers conduct assessments of pupil progress, identify learning needs and plan the next stages of learning as an essential part of their everyday activities. Assessment is quite rightly regarded as an essential process whereby we gain an understanding of the current state of pupil knowledge skills and understanding, the effectiveness of teaching approaches, and the need either to advance or modify our teaching. In so doing, an adherence to the principles of the SEN code of practice will enable teachers to gain more accurate and pertinent information.

Pupils gain an understanding of their progress in a number of ways. The feedback provided by the teacher or other adults is clearly important in informing pupils about how they are perceived to be progressing in their learning, and should also provide them with information about the things that they need to do in order to make further advances. Pupils are usually quite perceptive of their own engagement with the learning process. Most pupils recognise those subjects which they find easier than others or the ones which cause them difficulties. They are often aware of learning situations in which they feel confident and able to achieve, whilst others may be less conducive to progress. For example, some pupils feel more confident working in group situations than others. For some pupils with SEN, this may be related to an awareness of their limited communication or social skills, or it could be because they feel that other pupils do not perceive them as being able to make a viable contribution to the group. Unless they are encouraged to express their concerns, such pupils may simply tolerate a learning situation in which they feel uncomfortable and therefore fail to achieve their potential.

Teachers often recognise situations in which pupils feel less than comfortable and may be able to take measures to rectify such situations. However, pupils often tolerate a situation and put a brave face on it in order not to stand out from their peers and admit their difficulties. Effective teachers ensure that they provide opportunities for pupils to express how they feel about their own progress, the learning situations in which they operate, and those approaches, that can support their learning. This may be particularly challenging for some groups of pupils who have specific needs. For example, the cognitive differences of pupils with ASD mean that they are often limited in their ability to think about their own learning and have difficulty expressing their feelings in relation to their learning. Jordan and Powell (1990) explain the challenges pupils with ASD face in relation to 'metacognition' (learning how to learn) but recommend that we do not shy away from attempting to teach reflective skills, but rather that we exploit every opportunity within the curriculum for promoting the ability to 'learn how to learn'.

Pupil self-assessment is most useful when used alongside the teacher's own assessment procedures as a means of adding information or corroborating understanding and interpretation. However, the process of self-assessment needs the support of the teacher if it is going to be of real value. A set of principles needs to be established to ensure that both teachers and pupils benefit fully from pupil self-assessment procedures. These may be described as follows.

Accept that the teacher cannot know everything

In a busy classroom, it is not always possible to observe how well or badly pupils are performing at a given task. Pupils sometimes adopt strategies to give the appearance of being well engaged with an activity when in fact they are struggling to participate. Similarly, an overreliance upon pupil output in terms of the work they present on the pages of their books may not provide a true reflection of performance. Some pupils are adept at gaining information through other pupils and passing this off as their own understanding. Similarly, some pupils may be able to demonstrate a superficial understanding of concepts presented in a task whilst not fully comprehending the information that the teacher wishes them to attain. Teachers need to assure themselves of learning by questioning pupils and gaining their unique insights into the lesson. Of course, questioning is the most common form of assessment used by most teachers in primary schools. However, the nature of the questioning is critical. Much of the assessment questioning in schools focuses only upon the subject content and ignores the perceptions of the pupil or the conditions for learning.

Establish a clear focus

Pupils will be able to reflect upon their own performance only if they are clear about what they are supposed to have achieved. Naive questions such as *How do you feel you are doing in maths?* are not helpful in enabling pupils to provide the kind of detailed information that will assist the teacher. A much clearer focus is needed to encourage the pupil to consider specific aspects of learning. This is often better achieved by beginning an assessment conversation with a statement of intent. For example, the teacher may begin, *During this lesson I wanted you to use the ruler to measure the objects in your book and write down which were the longest and the shortest. Were you able to do this?* This question focuses the pupil on what was intended in the lesson. Such a question should be asked whilst the pupils have the teaching materials under consideration in front of them. In this situation, the teacher should not be prepared to accept a simple yes or no answer, but should expect the pupil to demonstrate the skill being assessed. If the pupil is clearly having difficulties with the task, the teacher should follow up by asking questions such as *What do you find most difficult about this task?* and *What can I do to make this task easier for you?*

Assess learning conditions as well as content

The assessment of pupils' work is clearly an essential task to be undertaken by the teacher. However, much is to be gained by focusing some attention on the conditions that pupils find most conducive to learning. Pupils are highly perceptive about other pupils with whom they work well and those who may create barriers to their personal performance. Similarly, they will often express a view on where in the class they work best and which resources are of help in learning effectively. Some pupils with SEN will experience difficulty in retaining information and benefit from being given instructions in more manageable units. Pupils need to know that it is appropriate to seek clarification and that the teacher does not regard this as a sign that they were not listening. Asking individual pupils about what helps them when information is presented may have a number of benefits. Some will find it easier to achieve the desired outcomes if visual support materials accompany verbal instructions. This may take the form of simple written instructions or could be presented in pictorial form. For some pupils, pairing with one of their peers who is given a specific task of reminding a pupil with SEN what needs to be done may reap rewards. Teachers are often effective at providing support to pupils in order to create optimal learning conditions. This is much more easily achieved when the pupils have confidence in the teacher and are assured that their own perceptions of the situation are taken fully into account.

Feedback to pupils in order to confirm their views

Gaining in confidence is, of course, dependent upon achieving positive outcomes. In discussing the needs of pupils with them and after this discussion
developing strategies to support learning, it is important to review how effective this has been. Teachers need to encourage pupils' self-assessment of
which actions have enabled them to work better. Reviewing the learning situation with a pupil can enable the teacher to emphasise the importance of getting the learning process right for a pupil who experiences difficulties. Pupils
value this emphasis upon their personal needs and will often respond positively when teachers enable them to recognise that they can make a valuable
contribution to identifying those conditions which encourage learning.
Similarly, if the pupil is continuing to experience difficulties, such a review can
be useful in reselecting strategies or modifying existing teaching approaches in
order to make learning more effective.

Encourage pupil-friendly approaches

Pupils will vary in their confidence in communicating their ideas or expressing opinions. It is essential that teachers have a range of alternative approaches
that support pupils in gaining effectiveness and confidence in self-assessment.
Enabling pupils to express their ideas through producing a poster or a comic
strip, or asking them to produce a mime or piece of drama may find favour
with some. Be aware of pupils who perceive themselves as having limited
skills that prevent them from expressing themselves through the written or
spoken word.

Demonstrate a commitment to action

An essential component of pupil involvement is ensuring that they recognise
the commitment that you as an individual teacher are making to their learning. Many pupils with SEN have become accustomed to failure and may have
simply accepted that they can not achieve the levels attained by their peers.
This can happen very early in the school lives of some pupils, and, unless
addressed, it will lead to increased negativity on the part of the pupil and a
lowering of expectations by adults. Too many pupils who are currently
labelled as having SEN have gained this status as a result of early failure to
engage with learning and a subsequent diminishing of confidence on the part
of both pupils and teachers. Teachers have an opportunity to communicate to
their pupils that they are able to learn, and that consideration will be given to
developing appropriate means to enable this to happen. This will best be
achieved when the teacher and pupil dialogue is founded upon mutual respect
and a commitment to take the actions upon which both parties are agreed. It

is true, of course, that this process has to be embraced by both the teacher and the pupil. Unfortunately, many pupils with SEN acquire a resistance to learning early in their primary school years. Some pupils who have experienced negative approaches to their learning and have had their perceived lack of ability reinforced by teachers who have not given sufficient attention to pupil interpretations of the challenges of the classroom, will have simply given up or adopted negative patterns of behaviour. Effective teachers give a commitment to addressing such negativity by building positive relationships with pupils and valuing the insights which they can provide about their own learning needs and the teaching approaches which best address these. Pupils will quickly recognise teachers who give a commitment to actions that are supportive of their learning. They will be equally adroit in challenging those teachers who fail to recognise the necessity of such actions.

Target setting

The SEN code of practice (2001) advises that pupils should be involved in the devising and management of their own individual education plans (IEPs) and the targets set within this (DfES, 2001a para. 3:7). Pupils need to be clear about their own targets if they are to move toward their successful achievement. The way in which they interpret these targets is particularly important. They must, of course, be clear about the intentions of the teacher. This means knowing not only what it is that they are working to achieve, but, equally important, what benefits will have been gained when the target is reached. Pupils need to see what is in this for them. They are far more likely to be motivated when they can see that the targets toward which they are working, when achieved, will bring benefits to them as individuals.

In discussing targets with pupils, it is important that they are clear about not only what it is you are hoping they will achieve, but also how you intend to get there. In order for targets to be worthwhile they must demand effort on the part of the learners, and teachers must ensure that once the targets are achieved pupils will be able to recognise that they can do something that they previously had not achieved. Apprehension about learning is common in pupils with SEN. This is why it is essential to discuss the targets within an IEP not only in terms of what they are, but also with respect to how pupils will be supported in their achievement. Spending time with pupils to anticipate what they may find difficult and discuss how obstacles may be overcome can only be beneficial. Such a discussion will not only increase the confidence of the pupil, but also enable the teacher to anticipate difficulties and to be well prepared for them. Similarly, discussion of targets within an IEP ensures that the pupil is clear about how important the teacher regards these as being.

For some pupils, the ability to engage in discussion may be inhibited as a result of language or communication difficulties. In some instances, the use of augmentative forms of communication, such as signs or symbols, may be essential to enable individual pupils to gain access to many aspects of their learning. If a pupil is used to using some form of augmentative or supported communication, it is essential that this is maintained during all processes of learning or assessment. Pupils may also be encouraged to express their ideas through their own preferred media, which could include drawing, writing or making their own audio recordings. For pupils who lack confidence in conversations with adults, this may be a means of both protecting them from potentially stressful situations and enabling them to make choices about how they communicate their ideas and feelings.

Regular reviewing of progress toward targets should engage pupils in a discussion which not only ensures that they can see how well they are doing, but also acknowledges the extra support that the teacher has provided to them. A discussion about the efficacy of procedures will again encourage pupils to appreciate the additional input that they are receiving, and communicate the value that the teacher places upon this relationship. When reviewing progress, it is important to recognise that target setting is a complex process. This inevitably means that sometimes targets will not be achieved or progress will be much slower than anticipated. When this is the case, pupils will require additional support and will benefit from an opportunity to analyse how the learning experience feels for them. Acknowledgement that a target may have been overambitious and discussion about this can ensure that pupils do not regard themselves as failures, or develop a more negative attitude toward the learning experience. The language used in such a discussion is critical. Emphasising where progress has been made, prior to considering areas of difficulty, will enable pupils to recognise their personal achievements and to be more likely to face challenges on the basis of these. The following case study illustrates the involvement of a pupil in target setting and reviewing progress.

> At a recent review of her progress, it was suggested that Natasha, a Year 2 pupil with learning difficulties, needed to concentrate on improving her skills of sociability. Natasha has few friends and does not like to share materials or join in group work. At times, this makes her quite isolated in the class. Natasha's teacher, Jenny realises that Natasha is likely to improve her sociability only if she is encouraged to see that this will be of benefit to herself. She also recognises that Natasha is unlikely to move quickly from being a social isolate to being able to relate well to everyone in the class.
>
> Jenny presents Natasha with a set of photographs of some of the other pupils in the class. She asks Natasha which of these classmates she likes most. Natasha indicates two girls whom she sometimes sits with during circle time. Jenny then asks Natasha to choose a game that they sometimes play in class, and when she has done this, Jenny talks to her about why she likes this game and how it is played.
>
> Jenny explains to Natasha that she wants her to learn to play the game better by playing with one of the two girls that she selected as people she likes. She

tells Natasha that she would like her to do this every morning just before lunchtime for 5 minutes. Jenny explains that by playing this game with the other girl, she will be making friends and that this is important for both Natasha and Jenny. Natasha agrees to try this idea.

Over the next few weeks, Natasha plays the game with the other girl. Sometimes this goes well, and on other occasions Natasha does not want to play or spoils the game. Every day at lunchtime, Jenny talks to Natasha about how she feels about playing the game, and asks the other girl to tell Natasha what she enjoys about playing with her. Jenny provides a simple chart on which Natasha is able to record with a smiling or frowning face how each day's game has gone. This chart is used as a focus for discussion at the end of each week.

Review procedures

There is an obligation to ensure that pupils with SEN have their progress reviewed on a regular basis. For some pupils this will entail attendance at a formal annual review as defined in the SEN code of practice (2001). This code encourages the involvement of pupils in the annual review, and it is important that schools develop policies on how this may best be achieved. Teachers need to consider pupil involvement in this process in three distinct phases, before, during and after the review.

Before the review, pupils need to be properly prepared for the experience that they are about to have in the review process. Pupils will be acutely aware that an important meeting is being convened specifically to discuss them and will often see this as being focused upon their personal difficulties. Care needs to be taken when choosing the language with which to discuss the review process with pupils. If teachers concentrate only on the fact that this meeting is being held because the individual pupil is having problems, they are likely to increase tensions and anxieties in the pupil. If pupils can be helped to see the review as a meeting during which they will be able to report on the positive actions taken since the last review and the progress that they have made, they are far more likely to adopt a positive attitude. Ideally, the review may be seen as a celebration of achievement, though often this is difficult to achieve, as the individuals concerned are likely to be aware that they are not performing as well as some of their peers.

Prior to the review, the pupil needs to be provided with clear and specific information about the purpose of the meeting, who will be there and why they will be there. The Children Act 2004 has acknowledged the stress which pupils often feel when confronted with several professionals from different services gathered together to discuss their needs. The concept of the lead professional has, to some extent, been developed to ensure a coordinated response eliminating the need for overwhelming meetings, which may be intimidating to the individual. However, there are bound to be apprehensions on the part of pupils and teachers must play an important role in supporting them through this process.

Pupils can be supported in this preparation stage by being asked to prepare their own views and ideas about what they would like to present to the meeting. An opportunity for pupils to present their own ideas should not be undervalued. For some pupils, the period before a review can become a useful period of reflection and assessment during which they are enabled to consider their own progress, achievements and continuing needs. Pupils may be encouraged to present their ideas in a visual format, maybe through producing a poster or some other form of display. Hayes (2004) illustrates, for example, the value of visual annual reviews in promoting positive participation. In a forum such as an annual review, it is helpful if pupils can express their own ideas about actions that have helped them overcome difficulties. Teachers might choose to help pupils to prepare not only an account of the positive things which have been achieved by them, but also examples of the actions taken by teachers or others that have been beneficial. Honesty demands that teachers also recognise that sometimes pupils will want to make comments about things that have not been successful or helpful. Here again an important role can be played in enabling pupils to select the language to use to express their views in a way that, whilst expressing an opinion, will be acceptable to the assembled professionals.

Some schools have used role-play in order to prepare pupils for the formality of the annual review meeting. In other instances, use has been made of video recordings of actual review meetings, though, of course, these need to be carefully managed in order to ensure that confidentiality issues are effectively managed. Decisions about this level of preparation and the approaches to be used will inevitably depend upon the confidence and preferences of the individuals concerned. During this preparation stage, it is important that pupils are afforded an opportunity to discuss how they wish to participate in the review. Some will choose not to attend, but may still be encouraged to produce materials, which the teacher can present on their behalf. Some might wish to attend but to have the teacher or another known adult speak for them, whilst others will have the confidence to speak for themselves.

A lack of preparation for participation in reviews is likely to leave pupils frustrated and possibly embarrassed. This phase of the review process is probably the most important in ensuring that pupils feel valued and maintain confidence in the adults who are responsible for their support.

During the review, pupils will need the support of a known adult. This is likely to be a class teacher or TA. Pupils will feel less daunted if they are confident that the people in the meeting are there to support them and to adopt a friendly tone. In most instances, a primary pupil is unlikely to feel comfortable sitting through the whole of a review meeting. If pupils are given a dedicated slot within the meeting, adults need to respect this as a period for them and to allow them the time to express themselves in whatever manner has been selected. The teacher or other named adult will need to act as a prompt and to ensure that positive feedback is constantly used to maintain the confidence of the pupil. Sometimes the teacher will want to interpret or clarify points, but should, wherever possible, avoid taking over the session and detracting from the pupil's own voice. Similarly, there will be times when the adult needs to help pupils understand questions that may be posed by the professionals present in the meeting. Pupils need to be given time to respond and to feel that their views are being fully considered.

In an ideal situation, once pupils leave the meeting, time should be given to discussing what has been learned by listening to their views. The involvement of pupils in annual reviews has, in some instances, been marred by tokenistic practice and has been nothing more than an appeasement of the requirements of legislation. Teachers can play an important role in fostering a philosophy of children's rights by ensuring that their professional colleagues take pupil views seriously, and by maintaining the views of the pupil at the centre of discussions in the meeting.

After the review, it is important that the earliest opportunity is found to discuss the meeting with the pupil concerned. This is often best begun with some reflection on how pupils felt about their own contribution. During the meeting, decisions will have been made and these need to be communicated to the pupils and discussed with them. For example, if specific actions have been agreed or targets set, the pupil will need to be clear about what these are and should be involved in a discussion about how they may be addressed. This may also be a good time to reflect on how the whole process has been managed. Do pupils have a view about how annual reviews might be managed in the future to make the process more valuable to them? Could they be better prepared? What have they learned through personal involvement?

The review process can be stressful and at times perceived as a negative experience by many pupils. Teachers can alleviate some of the anxiety and enable pupils to feel that they are respected through annual review procedures.

Michael in Year 5, is a friendly and enthusiastic pupil who likes school, but has difficulty with literacy and exhibits immature spoken language skills. He sometimes has difficulty with understanding instructions and with short-term memory. At his last annual review, it was suggested that Michael should work on two specific areas:

- to gain confidence in expressing himself in group situations
- to improve his memory through the introduction of a notebook system and a personal diary.

Michael's teacher has worked on these priorities with him for the past year and will support him in the forthcoming annual review. In order to do this, for the three weeks leading up to the review, Michael's teacher spends one lunchtime each week going through the work which Michael has accumulated over the year. This includes his notebook and diary and various pieces of work which he has collected in a portfolio. During these sessions, Michael is encouraged to talk about those things which have helped him to improve over the year and to select pieces of work which demonstrate his improvement.

Michael's teacher explains to him what will happen in the review. He explains who will be there and why they are meeting. These people, he explains are really interested to see how well Michael has done this year and to hear what he thinks about the work he has done. Michael, working with the teacher, produces a poster which illustrates the good things he has done in relation to the priorities set at the last review. Once the poster is completed, Michael shows this to a group of his friends, talking about the contents of the poster and letting them see his work. His friends are very encouraging and interested in what he has done.

During the review, Michael is able to show the poster to the gathered professionals and tell them what it illustrates. He gives them copies of his work, and his teacher explains how this demonstrates the progress that Michael has made. Michael is asked a couple of questions and is helped in answering these by his teacher.

After the review, Michael's teacher meets with him and praises him for the presentation in the meeting. He explains the decisions which were made in the meeting and reassures Michael that everyone is pleased with the progress he has made and impressed by his contribution to the meeting.

Teacher listening skills

Much of what has been discussed in this chapter has placed an emphasis upon the rights of pupils with SEN to have a voice in their education. Such a philosophy does not find favour in all quarters and will succeed only if it is built upon a commitment of respect for the individual. Listening to pupils does not mean that teachers always have to agree with their interpretation of a situation or, indeed, respond in order to meet pupil demands. As professional adults, we value the skills of respect, negotiation and understanding of different opinions that characterise the democratic process. These skills need to be learned, and if we do not begin by encouraging them in schools, we are less likely to maintain the democratic processes that most of us treasure.

In respecting the views of pupils, teachers need to be supported in developing active listening skills. Teachers must recognise that simply listening to pupils may often not be enough to convince them that their views are truly sought and respected. It is important to work with pupils to engender an ethos of trust through demonstrating that pupil views, where appropriate, can lead to actions to effect change for the better in pupils' lives. Many pupils who have become disaffected with education have had negative experiences of learning in school, where they believe that their own ideas and opinions have seldom been listened to and rarely respected. Teachers can do much to alleviate this situation.

Key questions and issues for reflection

- What opportunities are currently provided for pupils to be involved in assessing their own performance?
- What actions do I as a teacher take to enable pupils to see that I respect their ideas and opinions?
- How supportive of pupil views are current special needs procedures in school such as target setting or review procedures?
- What strategies are available to enable pupils to become part of this process?
- Are there changes to my practice which would enable pupils with SEN to gain confidence with regard to their perceptions of their own learning needs?

Conclusion

Teachers often underestimate the abilities of pupils to express their ideas and communicate a view of their own learning. It is clear from research evidence and through the experiences of teachers who have given a commitment to pupil involvement that pupils are certainly capable of making a significant contribution to the assessment of their own learning needs and the formulation of teaching ideas. All pupils appreciate being respected and having their ideas and opinions considered. This applies as much to those labelled as having SEN as to others in the class. Whilst some of the pupils in your class may lack confidence or have difficulty in communicating their ideas, it is clear that they will not improve in these areas unless they are provided with sufficient opportunities to try. Whilst, as a new teacher, you will want to ensure that you can maintain control over your class, you are likely to find this easier when you afford opportunities for pupils to express themselves and feel that they are part of the decision-making processes in your classroom.

8 Looking beyond school

Overview

This chapter will address the following issues:

- pupils' lives outside the classroom
- parent partnerships
- supporting transitions
- preparing for out-of-school experiences
- recognising and celebrating out-of-school achievements.

Introduction

Whilst this book focuses upon inclusion in primary mainstream schools, consideration of effective inclusion must look beyond the classroom and school. As a newly qualified teacher, you will inevitably be focusing upon establishing yourself in your new classroom; developing relationships with pupils, colleagues and other professionals; and exploring diverse teaching and learning strategies. However, in order to meet individual needs effectively it is also important to consider pupils' needs beyond the classroom and school context. The *Every Child Matters* agenda emphasises the commitment to the 'whole child', and as schools strive to create an environment and ethos that promotes the five key features of this agenda, so it is imperative that this include involvement and partnerships with parents and carers, and consider aspects of pupils' lives outside school.

This chapter explores key features of pupils' lives beyond the classroom and considers aspects relating to your role. One key element of this role is to support and develop partnerships with parents and carers. Chapter 6 explored the need for developing partnerships with colleagues, other professionals and pupils; equally importantly, you will need to develop and nurture partnerships with parents and carers in order to consider the needs of the whole child. A second aspect relates to transitions pupils will make from your class; these may include transitions between classes at the end of an academic year, transitions from one key stage to the next, and the transition to secondary school, where careful planning and support will be vital. Thirdly, preparation for out-of-school experiences will be essential for all pupils, with some pupils requiring specific support in order for them to be able to participate successfully. Finally, recognition and celebration of out-of-school achievements is another feature of life beyond the classroom that needs to be valued in the classroom.

Developing partnerships with parents and carers

Whilst you concentrate upon developing effective relationships with individual pupils in the classroom, consideration of their lives outside the classroom and those involved in their whole development is an integral part of your role. Pupils bring to the classroom all of their experiences from outside the school. Developing a good relationship with parents is a key professional skill that will benefit all involved in a pupil's education. This is especially important where a pupil has SEN. The SEN code of practice (DfES, 2001a) emphasises the importance of partnerships with parents in promoting cooperation between all those involved with pupils with SEN, stating that *parents hold key information and have a critical role to play in their children's education. They have unique strengths, knowledge and experience to contribute to the shared view of a child's needs and the best ways of supporting them* (p16). The code suggests that effective partnership with parents enhances the work of professionals, and that it is essential that professionals work actively with parents and value their contribution to the teaching and learning partnership.

Working with and supporting parents is therefore an essential feature of inclusive practice; relationships with parents will of course differ according to needs and will require effective communication skills in order to promote a true sense of partnership. Teacher/parent partnerships will vary and may include the need to provide parents with support, involving parents in working toward individual targets, utilising parents' expertise in relation to their child and strategies they find useful at home, and working together to help pupils to generalise their learning.

Providing support

Parents and other family members of pupils with SEN will be affected by their needs, strengths and difficulties in different ways. Parents may need support for a variety of reasons. Initial identification of SEN and, for some pupils and families, receiving that diagnosis can cause high levels of anxiety and emotional stress. Identification of individual needs and/or diagnoses of specific conditions or disorders may occur at any time during a pupil's school career but usually occur during the Foundation Stage and primary years. Parents and carers may need support when the initial concerns about a pupil are 'triggered', support as the school assesses individual needs and responds with 'school action', support when other agencies and professionals are involved at 'school action plus', support through formal assessment and possibly the issuing of a statement of SEN, and finally support if any formal diagnosis is made. Throughout this process, the class teacher is often the key professional to whom parents will look to for support, advice and information. As a newly qualified and less experienced teacher you will nevertheless find yourself in a role that requires you to provide support for parents. It will be essential for you to work closely with the SENCO in order to develop good communication skills and the ability to offer advice to parents in a constructive and supportive manner. The following case study provides an example of how a newly qualified teacher set up a supportive system for a parent whose child had recently received the diagnosis of ASD.

Supporting parents

Jack is a 6-year-old pupil in Year 1 of his local primary school. After various assessments during the Foundation Stage, during his first term of Year 1, Jack was identified as having ASD. This caused extreme anxiety for his mother (a single parent), who asked for a meeting with Jack's teacher, Ms Harrison, to discuss the implications of this diagnosis.

Ms Harrison had an informal discussion with Jack's mother and suggested that they meet together with the SENCO and the TA supporting Jack in class. Jack already had an IEP, and his mother was keen to support Jack in relation to his targets. At this meeting, a number of issues were raised by Jack's mother:

- the need for information about ASD
- the need for information about strategies to support Jack's learning
- the lack of communication from Jack about his experiences at school
- the need for reassurance about Jack's behaviour and progress each day.

After this meeting, Ms Harrison, the SENCO and the TA identified ways of supporting Ms Harrison and presented their ideas at a subsequent meeting as follows:

- The SENCO suggested a list of books for Jack's mother to read, and provided her with details of the National Autistic Society and the local ASD society helpline and parent support groups. In addition, the SENCO provided reading materials for Ms Harrison and the TA.
- Ms Harrison discussed Jack's targets at school and, together with Jack's mother, the SENCO and the TA, identified one target that Jack's mother could support at home. This target related to social/communication skills involving asking for help when needed. Ms Harrison discussed strategies for develop-

ing this skill at home, and the TA provided a visual cue card, identical to one used in school, for Jack to indicate when he needs 'help' at home. This provided a consistent support strategy between the school and home context.

- The main source of anxiety for Jack's mother was her lack of knowledge about his day due to his lack of communication skills. Jack's mother requested daily contact with Ms Harrison, although it was decided that this was not practical. Ms Harrison suggested that she could meet with Jack's mother once a week and that the TA could meet with her at the end of each day to provide information about Jack's day. This face-to-face contact was essential during this period.

As Jack made progress and his mother came to terms with his diagnosis, her need for daily face-to-face contact reduced. Ms Harrison then put in place a home–school communication book, in which achievements, progress and behaviour could be recorded each day. This book provided Jack's mother with information about his day, which she could then use to try to encourage him to communicate. Similarly, Jack's mother recorded events at home that could be used at school to prompt communication from Jack. In time, Jack began to contribute to the home–school book; for example, he used symbols to record what he did at the weekend in order to tell his 'news' to the class. The home–school book became a valuable tool for Jack's mother, teacher, TA and Jack.

This case study illustrates the sensitive, thoughtful and practical approach taken to support Jack's mother after his diagnosis.

Working toward targets

As in the preceding case study, many parents of pupils with SEN wish to support their children in working toward individual targets. IEP review meetings provide the vehicle for sharing information about targets with parents and the pupil. This meeting may provide opportunities for discussing how parents could support their child's learning toward specific targets, as in the following case study.

Supporting targets

Tina, a Year 5 pupil, has individual needs relating to numeracy and literacy and is supported through school action. At Tina's IEP review meeting, one target set for Tina was *to practise addition in real-life contexts*. Tina's teacher gave her parents examples of how this might be achieved at school and discussed how they could provide opportunities for working toward this target at home. Tina's parents agreed that they would encourage Tina to add totals in a range of contexts, including shopping and fast food bills. Tina's teacher showed her parents the methods of addition that they had found to be most useful for Tina in order to ensure a consistent strategy.

Sharing targets with parents and discussing how parents might actively support learning in key areas may have benefits for both the pupil and the parents; parents feel involved as partners in their child's learning and individual pupils are provided with more opportunities to consolidate their learning. The key to this approach is to develop effective communication skills and to encourage parents to become involved in working toward individual targets – this may seem obvious, but it does not always happen, some parents remaining largely unaware of individual targets and what they could do to support their child's learning.

Utilising parents' expertise

Whilst you will have a good understanding of individual pupils' strengths and needs, and you may have developed expertise in relation to specific needs and/or strategies, parents are usually the 'experts' in relation to their own child. As a teacher, you must develop flexible relationships with parents that acknowledge the expertise of all involved with the child. The TEACCH approach to ASD, for example, advocates various models of parent/professional relationships, which include viewing parents as trainees (requiring support and help) and parents as experts (offering essential information to professionals) with the aim of fostering mutual support between parents and professionals. Carpenter (2001) emphasises the need for teachers to recognise the individuality of parents and families, each of which will experience their own stresses and will have different levels of understanding and varying expectations of schools. The utilisation of parental expertise in support of pupils in the primary classroom will be possible only when you are prepared to try and see situations not only from your own point of view, but also from the perspective of the parent or carer. As Carpenter states, it is essential that, as a teacher, you demonstrate respect, genuineness and empathy toward parents who may be having difficulties coming to terms with or understanding the implications of their child's SEN. Building upon the work of earlier researchers (Cunningham and Davis, 1985), Carpenter advocates a 'consumer' model of providing support to families. This, he says is based upon

- a shared sense of purpose
- a willingness to negotiate
- sharing of information
- shared responsibility
- joint decision making and accountability. (Carpenter, 2001, p278)

None of these elements will be achieved unless you are willing to listen to parents or carers and learn from their responsibilities. This requires a certain amount of confidence on your part, and this will be gained only with time and a considerable investment of your own energy in making a commitment to the families of pupils in your class. Parents have unique insights into the needs, likes, dislikes, motivations and moods of their children. Teachers who choose to disregard this critical source of information are less likely to address the needs of pupils who challenge. This is not to suggest that parents are always right, or that you will be able to respond to every request that comes your way. However, parents will respect your professionalism when they are able to see that you are prepared to listen to their ideas and make professional judgements that are informed by an understanding of their needs.

Many parents or carers will have specific expertise, which you may be able to utilise in your classroom. Some will have specialist skills, possibly as musicians or in the use of computers; others will be effective in listening to children reading, telling stories or simply listening to children talking about their work. Such people provide a valuable resource, which many schools use effectively to support the teaching and learning process. Unfortunately, others are less proficient and, in some instances, unwilling to engage at this level of partnership. Pupils with SEN benefit from having good adult role models. Whilst you will play a major role in providing such an example, the introduction of other adults into the class may be an effective way of reinforcing the support which such pupils need.

Utilising parents' expertise may well enhance strategies and practice for an individual pupil, as illustrated in the following case study.

Utilising parents' expertise

Wayne is in Year 3 of his local primary school. He has a physical disability affecting his limbs and has difficulty with gross and fine motor skills. The school has support from the physiotherapy service, who have provided a programme of daily exercises for Wayne to complete at school and home. An LSA works with Wayne on a one-to-one basis to complete his exercises each day. The LSA has recently reported to his teacher that Wayne has become reluctant to complete his exercises and is complaining that it is 'boring' and he would rather play outside. Despite her efforts to make the sessions fun, Wayne is becoming increasingly uncooperative.

Wayne's teacher invited his parents for an informal discussion to explain the situation and to ask how his parents motivate him to complete his exercises at home. Wayne's mother came to school for a chat, and she explained how they motivated and encouraged Wayne to complete his exercises at home, including involvement of his brother, listening to music on his MP3 player as he exercises, watching TV while he exercises and rewarding him with extra time on the computer. Following this meeting, Wayne's teacher and the LSA discussed Wayne's exercise programme with the physiotherapist, and the following strategies were tried:

- A peer (an exercise buddy) was involved of in some of the exercises – a team of buddies were asked to volunteer to join Wayne on a rota basis.

- It was agreed that Wayne could bring in his MP3 player and listen to music as he completed some of the exercises one day per week and that he could watch TV as he exercised for one day per week.
- A reward system was put in place to offer extra computer time for Wayne and his exercise buddy.

With these added motivators, Wayne began to cooperate, and he particularly enjoyed having an exercise buddy. Whilst it was acknowledged that eventually Wayne might become bored again in the future, it was agreed that all those involved with the exercise programme would work together to maintain his motivation.

This case study illustrates the importance and value of involving parents and asking for their advice in order to meet individual needs. Parents are rich sources of information about their child, and when their expertise is utilised, the benefits are felt by all. If pupils have a particular disorder or condition, parents will often have detailed knowledge about their individual needs and may also be able to provide suggestions about strategies that are helpful at home and that may also be useful in school. Involving parents and developing a partnership approach to meeting individual needs is an essential part of effective practice and one that you should seek to develop.

Generalising learning and developing consistent approaches

A further area for involving parents and carers relates to encouraging pupils to generalise what they have learnt beyond the classroom context and to develop consistent approaches across settings. Pupils with SEN may need support to apply and generalise what they have learnt. We know, for example, that pupils with ASD have particular needs in this area due to 'compartmentalising' their learning and failing to see the connections between their learning in one context and another. Pupils with learning difficulties may require additional opportunities to rehearse skills learnt in school in other contexts in order to apply their knowledge and skills. Teachers who involve parents and carers in helping pupils to apply and to generalise their learning will actively foster the teacher/parent partnership and will experience benefits for the pupil. In addition, consistency of approach across school and home settings can strengthen an approach and result in more positive outcomes. The following case study illustrates how one teacher and a TA worked together with a pupil's parents in order to help the pupil to generalise and apply his learning in the classroom to broader contexts and to develop a consistent approach to managing his behaviour.

Generalising learning and developing consistency

Billy, in Year 2, and has individual needs relating to literacy and behaviour; he is supported through school action and has IEP targets that focus upon developing reading skills and social skills to improve his behaviour. Billy has some TA support, both one to one and in a small group. Two of the current targets that he is working toward are:

- to use initial sounds and picture cues to attempt unfamiliar words
- to take turns with one peer in structured activities.

Billy's teacher and the TA developed a range of activities through which he could work toward these targets with the TA; opportunities for working towards the targets were also identified in the teacher's class planning; for example, Billy was supported by the TA to take turns with one peer to play a numeracy game during a maths lesson.

As it became clear which strategies and resources were helpful to Billy, his teacher and the TA met with his parents to share their ideas and to encourage Billy to work toward these targets at home. Billy's parents were keen to help him with his reading but were unsure how best to help. In addition, Billy still needed support to take turns with a peer at school, and although he was making progress in this area, his mother reported that he could not take turns or share with his siblings at home and that this caused behavioural outbursts.

The teacher and the TA discussed the reading strategies that were being used at school and showed Billy's parents how to help him to look for cues to attempt to read unfamiliar words. They also suggested that Billy and his mother/father take turns with Billy to read, to practise taking turns in a structured way. The TA also showed Billy's parents some of the games and activities that she had been using at school to encourage Billy to take turns with a peer; many of these resources had been developed by the TA to incorporate Billy's interests in football and planets. In addition, a 'your turn' cue card had been introduced by the TA to provide a concrete, visual cue to reinforce whose turn it is – Billy and his peer were taught to pass the 'your turn' card to each other. It was agreed that Billy could borrow one of the resources each week to take home; the TA also provided a 'your turn' card for use at home. Billy's parents agreed that they would encourage him to take turns, with one sibling, using these resources and supported by his mother or father. A record of his progress toward this target was devised, including planet stickers, so that Billy, his teacher, TA and parents could monitor his progress and achievements. It was agreed that when Billy achieved the target he would be taken on a visit to the local space centre.

All of the previous case studies provide examples of how you might engage with and support parents and carers. These examples also illustrate key themes that emerge: sharing information, mutual support and consistency of approach are all essential. These need to be built upon the development of mutual respect and a commitment to develop a partnership with parents that is meaningful and practical. Pupils will interpret your relationship with their parents or carers, and this will inevitably influence the ways in which they behave both at school and home. If pupils believe that there are difficulties between you and their parents or carers, they have an opportunity to exploit this negative relationship, and this can potentially lead to conflict.

Key questions and issues for reflection

- How do I support parents and carers?
- How do I involve parents and carers in supporting their child's learning?
- What strategies am I using successfully at school that could be introduced at home to generalise learning and to achieve consistent approaches?
- Do I ask parents for information or for suggestions about their child that could be useful to support individual needs at school?
- What are my professional development needs in this area?

Transitions

Transitions between classes, key stages and schools are important times for all pupils. A focus upon transition issues is clearly indicated in *Excellence and Enjoyment: A Strategy for Primary Schools* (DfES, 2003b): *We know that any transition from one stage of learning to another presents challenges for teachers* (p43). Transitions may also present difficulties for pupils, and these may be exacerbated for those with SEN. Such times may evoke anxiety and fears for pupils and their families, who are uncertain about the changes ahead or apprehensive about moving from the security of a known situation or familiar adults. Studies show that transition issues raise varying problems and challenges. For example, Sanders et al. (2005) suggest that the transition from Foundation Stage to Key Stage 1 raises a number of issues for children, parents and staff, and that pupils with special educational needs are among the most likely to experience difficulties and will require greater support. Mortimer (2001) suggests that the communication between teachers, pupils and families at times of transition is an essential component of enabling the movement between classes or phases to proceed without difficulty. As a teacher, you will be expected by parents and carers to have insights about the next stage of provision for their child. This expectation can be met only if you ensure that you are informed and make the effort to find out what the awaiting provision is like.

You can do much to support a pupil with SEN through the process of transition. Simply communicating to a pupil and providing reassurance about coming events can help. Most schools encourage visits at times of transfer from primary to secondary provision, but few have such procedures in place for transfer between classes within a school. This simple act of enabling a pupil to spend time in a class to which they will be moving can save a lot of anxiety and be reassuring to both pupil and staff. In considering the conditions which influence transitions, Polat et al. (2002) emphasise the importance of making effective use of peer support. Pupils do not move from one educational setting to another alone (an exception to this could be transfer to a special school or a school in another area). Developing peer support mechanisms can be important in enabling pupils to feel comfortable about changes in situation, particularly if friends or classmates are well briefed about providing appropriate levels of support. Remember that staff as well as pupils may have apprehension during times of transition. If you have a pupil with SEN in your class and the next teachers to receive this pupil are unfamiliar with such needs, they may be uncomfortable about the transfer of the pupil. You should consider the kinds of procedures that may alleviate anxiety in this situation. This may include a range of measures including:

- the production of written pen portraits of a pupil, outlining the pupil's needs, likes, dislikes and preferred learning style for the receiving staff
- the development of a transition pack for pupils containing pictures and details of the class to which they will be moving
- the establishment of a peer supporter who will befriend a pupil through a period of transition
- the setting up of a meeting between the pupil and the receiving teacher in a familiar environment, such as the pupil's current classroom.

The following case study illustrates how one teacher supported the transition of a pupil with SEN from his class to a receiving teacher.

Transition

Alex is a Year 2 pupil who next term will be moving from the infant school to a local junior school. He is currently in a class of 29 pupils, 27 of whom will move with him in September. Alex has Down's syndrome and general learning difficulties. Whilst he has been very happy at his infant school, he is always apprehensive at times of change and has taken time to settle whenever he has changed class. Alex's teacher, Bob, knows that the move to a different school is likely to be unsettling for Alex and has therefore taken a number of steps to ensure that he is well supported. He began planning for the change of school very early. In March, Bob visited the junior school and met with the teacher who will be receiving Alex in September. He took with him a written pen portrait of Alex and some samples of his work. During this visit, Bob emphasised that Alex was a keen pupil who worked hard in his class and that, although his academic attainment was not as that of good as most of his peers, he had definite learning strengths. He demonstrated these strengths by showing work that Alex had completed that term.

Early in the summer term, Alex began talking to the whole class about the move to the junior school. He showed them photographs of the school and some of the work which pupils in Year 3 had produced and which had been provided by their teacher. He emphasised some of the exciting opportunities which pupils would have in their new school. In May, Bob visited the junior school again, this time taking Alex and one of his friends who would be transferring with him. They visited the school toward the end of an afternoon and joined the Year 3 class to listen to their teacher telling a story. For this visit, the Year 3 teacher had prepared her class each of whom told the visiting infant pupils what their favourite thing about the junior school was.

Back at school the next day, Alex and his friend were encouraged to talk to the whole class about their visit and to remember as many as possible of the Year 3 pupils' favourite things. Bob told the class that Alex was now an 'expert' on the new school, and that he would be able to help them all when they transfer. In July, the whole class visited the junior school, and Alex and his friend were encouraged to tell all the pupils what to expect. At the end of term, each pupil in the class wrote their own short biography, which they would take with them to their new class in September. Bob arranged with the Year 3 teacher to use these biographies with the pupils several times during their first 2 weeks in the new class.

In the case study above, we can see how Bob has provided effective support for both Alex and his new teacher. Alex is being given not only reassurance, but also some responsibility in informing his classmates about the coming transition. In this way, he gains confidence by recognising the positive aspects of the impending move and realising that he is in a knowledgeable position. He has also gained confidence by getting to know the teacher for next term and has a partner for transition who will give him extra confidence.

Pupils with SEN will of course vary in their requirements for transition support, depending upon their individual needs; some groups of pupils may be particularly vulnerable, however. For example, pupils with ASD who often rely upon routine and who find variation to routines stressful may require support for transitions in addition to that provided for the majority of pupils. The DfES (2002) 'Guidance to Good Practice' for pupils with ASD provides pointers in relation to supporting transitions. The guidance recognises the importance of supporting transitions for pupils with ASD and provides a number of useful case studies to illustrate levels of support; for example, the Footsteps project in Sheffield supports preschool children in their transition to school as follows:

A nursery-aged child with Asperger's Syndrome was supported by a number of visits by his Support Worker from the project, to allow him to experience routines like playtimes, and assembly. A STEPS (Services for Autism) assistant will then give additional support on a weekly basis (for the first year) to ensure the correct and appropriate use of relevant teaching strategies such as visual timetables and to help with resources and other possible issues, for example, behaviour.

Such an approach will clearly require close liaison with the early-years teacher, who in turn will need to feel confident in collaborating with the preschool key worker and support worker. The ability to work closely with others will be crucial for effective transitions for pupils with SEN. In addition to those groups of pupils that we know to be vulnerable in this area, there will be individual pupils who also require carefully planned support. The following case study illustrates the development of a 'transition pack' for one pupil with ADHD and social, emotional and behavioural difficulties.

Supporting transitions

Andrew was diagnosed with ADHD during Year 3. Since then, his primary school has developed a number of strategies for supporting Andrew and for promoting positive behaviour, including the use of visual cue cards and rules, cue cards for Andrew to indicate when he is angry or feels he needs to leave the lesson, a 'feelings' colour wheel to help him to identify how he is feeling, buddy support, organisational strategies for starting and finishing tasks, and individual responsibilities to increase his self-esteem.

During the summer term of Year 6, Andrew's teacher, TA and the SENCO worked together with the SENCO and a TA who would be supporting Andrew from the secondary school which he would join in September. Andrew's teacher suggested that the TAs should liaise with each other and visit each of the settings in order to share information and ideas. The teacher offered to have the TA from the secondary school join some lessons on a weekly basis to get to know Andrew and to begin to develop a relationship with him. In addition, Andrew was taken on induction visits, additional to those made by his class, in order to become familiar with the setting and key adults such as the SENCO and his Year 7 tutor.

Andrew's teacher also suggested that the TA who had been supporting him during Year 6 should make up a transition pack comprising a pen picture of Andrew (with contributions from himself), outlines of support strategies they had found useful and copies of all resources used such as cue cards. The TA decided to make up two packs, one for his new school and one for Andrew and his family. Andrew was also given key information about his new school to add to his transition pack.

The aim of this transition support was to reassure Andrew and to establish some consistency of approach as he moved from primary to secondary school.

This case study illustrates good practice in relation to supporting a pupil who requires additional help with transition to secondary school. The class teacher and TA were keen to collaborate with the secondary school, as Andrew had made great progress and his self-esteem had improved, especially during Years 5 and 6. Together with his parents, they were keen to maintain this progress and to continue to enhance his self-esteem; in recognition that the transition was potentially stressful for Andrew, the teacher was willing to invite staff from the secondary school to observe her classroom practice and Andrew's responses.

> **Key questions and issues for reflection**
>
> - Which pupils in my class may need extra support through transition (either to another class or a different school)?
> - How familiar am I with the transition venue for my pupils?
> - What procedures can I put in place to support transition?
> - What information will receiving teachers need about pupils with SEN?

Preparing pupils with SEN for school visits

School visits are greeted with enthusiasm and excitement by most pupils. However, you should not assume that all pupils look forward to the experience as a positive opportunity. For some, the insecurity of the unfamiliar or not knowing what to expect can be worrying and in some instances traumatic. For example, some pupils with ASD who thrive on routine and an appreciation of the familiar may find difficulty in anticipating a day away from school. It may be necessary to commit time to preparation of pupils for such a visit if it is not to be a traumatic experience.

Similarly, if you want to ensure the best learning opportunities for all pupils during a school trip, early preparation is likely to be essential. Pupils with learning difficulties may find it hard to conceptualise the purpose of a visit or the expectations which you have of learning during such a trip. For example, if you are planning a trip to a museum, you should not assume that all of the pupils in your class will know what a museum is. This will depend upon pupils' previous experiences, and may possibly relate to the interest of their parents or carers. Some pupils will need not only an explanation of the purpose of such a visit, but also an explanation of the purpose and functioning of museums.

For some pupils, being away from school may mean that they are unsure how to behave. Remember that some of your pupils will behave at home very differently from in school. For pupils with behaviour difficulties to transfer their understanding of codes of behaviour from one venue to another will require guidance from you. Being on a field trip, particularly if this involves being out of doors, may be difficult for some pupils who are used to having a free run in open space. As a teacher, you must set the perameters within which you expect pupils to operate, and must apply your expectations consistently.

School visits can be very important in assisting all pupils, including those with learning difficulties, to build a real understanding of the world. History lessons in which you teach pupils about the Romans can be made very exciting and interesting, but actually visiting a Roman villa or handling Roman artefacts on a visit to a museum can help to bring history to life. Your visits will be most effective for all pupils, including those with SEN, if you plan carefully and prepare them for the experiences which you are going to provide. A few simple rules may assist in making the most of your school trip. Although not all pupils will require special provision, this checklist may save you some anxiety and problems on the day.

- Visit the venue before the trip to check on issues of access, including toilet facilities.
- Check to see if the venue provides information for pupils in specialist formats (such as large print for a pupil with a visual impairment).
- If a pupil needs enlarged print and none is available, take leaflets and other materials and make enlarged photocopies.
- Use photographs or artefacts before a visit to prepare pupils; this may address any anxieties in members of your class.
- Check on any need for medication, or dietary or other specialist needs which pupils may have well in advance of the event. You may need to make special provision to deal with these.
- Talk to the pupils about your expectations for behaviour on the visit.
- Brief adults who are supporting the visit about any special needs of pupils in your class. Ensure that they know exactly what you expect of them and talk to the pupils about the support which they will receive.
- Some pupils may be supported by additional visual materials that they take with them to indicate the events of the day. A visual timetable may be reassuring for some pupils (see the following case study).
- Consider allocating a 'buddy' for pupils who may be apprehensive. Make sure that this buddy is well briefed and is happy to fulfil this role.

Farm visit

Olive is taking her Year 1 class from a village school on a visit to a local farm as part of a project about the local community. She has arranged with the farmer to visit the dairy to see cows being milked, to see the pigs being fed and to walk around some of the fields to see both animals and crops. Before the trip, she visits the farm and talks to the farmer about the visit. She explains that among her pupils are one who uses a wheelchair and another with Asperger's syndrome, who may require a lot of encouragement and reassurance during the visit. The farmer takes her around the site of the visit and plans with Olive a route around the farm that will be easiest for a wheelchair user. He arranges to lay some boards across part of a path which is very soft and would cause difficulty for the chair. They also decide to avoid one particular field that would cause similar difficulty. Olive takes a number of photographs with a digital camera for use with her class.

Before the visit, Olive shows the class a DVD about life on a farm. She also makes a display with the photographs which she took during the earlier visit and talks to the class about this. On the afternoon before the visit, she goes through a sequence of what she expects to happen the next day. For her pupil with Asperger's syndrome, Barry, she has prepared a visual timetable of the day, using some of her photographs from the farm. She allocates a TA to work with this pupil and to stay with him throughout the visit.

During the visit Barry stays with the TA throughout. Every few minutes, the TA goes through his timetable with him, reassuring him about what will happen next. He is clearly unhappy in the dairy, so she takes him out for a while and talks to him about the morning, again using his timetable to indicate that he will soon be back in familiar surroundings.

Back in class, Olive talks to the pupils about what they have seen at the farm. The pupils are mostly very excited about the visit, which they have clearly enjoyed. Olive makes a particular point of praising Barry for his behaviour and for taking part in the trip.

In the preceding case study, Olive is well organised and her visit proceeds without problems. Excluding pupils from a visit on the grounds of their SEN is unacceptable and could constitute an infringement of equal opportunities. Such an exclusion would certainly have a negative impact upon a pupil's self-esteem and would give an unfortunate message about the ways in which a school values its pupils.

Key questions and issues for reflection

- Which pupils in my class may need additional support on a school visit?
- How will I prepare pupils with SEN so that they know what to expect on the visit?
- How familiar am I with the school's policy on visits?
- How will I brief adults supporting the visit on the needs of the pupils?

Recognition of out-of-school achievements

It is important to recognise that the learning taking place in school is only one part of the educational experiences which pupils gain. Pupils participate in a wide range of events, activities and other experiences, which broaden their understanding of the world and the communities in which they live and provide rich opportunities for learning. Many of the pupils within your class will belong to associations, such as Cub Scouts or Brownies; may attend sports clubs, religious or interest groups; and will certainly be involved in activities with family and friends. Through these activities, they will gain knowledge and understanding that is often different from, but complementary to, that which is taught in your classroom. You should recognise the value of pupil experiences out of school and learn to use these to your advantage and that of your class.

Some pupils with SEN may be able to excel at out-of-school activities even though they struggle with learning in class. Pupil self-esteem may be considerably enhanced if you not only recognise, but also celebrate this out-of-school

learning. All pupils need to know that, as their teacher, you are personally interested in them. Making time at the start of each day to talk about their interests
or what they have done since you last met demonstrates your interest in them
and also helps you to identify a range of learning opportunities. Many teachers
encourage pupils to bring to school things that provide evidence of personal
achievement outside school, such as swimming certificates, badges gained
through Brownies or sporting trophies, of which pupils are rightly proud. They
indicate application and also reflect a life in the community outside school that
we wish to encourage. A pupil with SEN may find difficulty in academic terms
but could well excel in activities outside school. For such pupils, this may provide a unique opportunity for you to support their self-esteem.

Colin is a Year 6 pupil who has been diagnosed with ADHD. He has difficulty
concentrating in class, and is restless and at times disruptive. Within the class, he
has few friends, and some pupils are wary of his unpredictability. Colin's academic attainment is poor, and he is very aware of his difficulty in most subjects. At
times, when he finds work too challenging, he becomes aggressive toward the
other pupils and occasionally toward adults in his class.

On Monday morning, Colin arrives in school with a large brown envelope,
which he shows to Gail, his teacher. In the envelope is a certificate and a medallion. Colin gained these by taking part in a sponsored run for a local charity event
to raise money for the Guide Dogs for the Blind Association.

After registration, Gail talks to the class, asking them about their weekend. She
shows the whole class Colin's certificate and medallion and asks him to tell
everyone how he gained these. Gail talks to the class about the importance of
doing things for other people and tells them how proud she is of Colin's achievement. Colin's certificate and medallion are displayed prominently in class so that
everyone can see them. Gail also informs the head teacher of Colin's achievement so that he receives a mention in assembly.

At lunchtime, Gail asks Colin if he would like to help her find out more about
how guide dogs are trained and work. Together, they spend half an hour on the
internet finding information, and downloading and printing pictures. Gail discovers that Colin's grandmother is blind, and that, although she does not have a
guide dog, Colin's family have made a commitment to raise funds to help other
blind people. Colin is clearly pleased to have this attention. Gail suggests that
tomorrow they can make some time to put the information together as a display
and asks him if, at the end of the week, he would like to talk to the whole class
about guide dogs.

On Friday, Colin shows his display and talks to the class for 5 minutes about
what he knows about guide dogs. The class is impressed with Colin's knowledge
and asks him lots of questions. Colin finishes the week feeling very pleased with
what he has achieved.

In the preceding case study, we see how a teacher has recognised the individuality of a pupil who is in danger of feeling excluded from his class. She promotes

his inclusion by drawing attention to a positive aspect of Colin's life and thus raises his self-esteem, whilst focusing the other pupils' attention on something about Colin with which they were unfamiliar. Such an action is unlikely to have a direct impact upon Colin's academic attainment, but does encourage him to feel better disposed toward the teacher, his classmates and school as a whole.

Schools should be at the hub of their local community. It is therefore vital that you are aware of what is happening within the locality of the school and of the ways in which the pupils engage with local activity. Armstrong (2003) has discussed the tensions between the need to promote citizenship, a critical part of the school curriculum, and the reality of the lives of people with disabilities or SEN. Whilst theories about citizenship and teaching it as a subject in schools are undoubtedly a welcome advance, this does not guarantee that pupils will engage in local activity. The role of the teacher here may be critical, and whilst you cannot and should not manipulate the lives of your pupils beyond the classroom, you may well wish to encourage greater social participation, which can enhance their lives. Sometimes, as a teacher, you may have opportunities to encourage pupils who are socially isolated and have few friends to become more outgoing and confident by supporting them in becoming involved in out-of-school clubs or activities. For example, many teachers have made contact with local groups on behalf of a pupil who wishes to join but does not have the confidence to do so without support. Sometimes this may mean asking a parent who takes a pupil regularly to a football club, dancing lessons or some other activity, if they would be willing to introduce a pupil who is keen to attend but lacks the confidence. As pupils gain in confidence through association with others outside school, they often become more settled in school. If you have pupils with SEN, particularly if this is in the form of a disability, they and their parents may not feel that they would gain admission to local organisations. However, most youth organisations do have equal-opportunities policies and will welcome pupils with disabilities. Some, such as the Scout Movement, have trained officials who can advise and support activity. Many schools keep directories of local organisations and key people who can assist. As a new teacher, particularly if you have started teaching in an area with which you are unfamiliar, you should try to familiarise yourself with such information and should also be aware of the details, which you can obtain from the pupils themselves.

Key questions and issues for reflection

- How familiar am I with the activities with which pupils engage outside school?
- What opportunities do I provide for a celebration of these activities?
- When do I make time for pupils to share information about their lives out of school?

Conclusion

Throughout this chapter, we have emphasised the need to establish effective partnerships and maintain channels of communication. Good partnerships with pupils, families and outside agencies can often prevent difficulties and enable you to gain insights into the most effective ways of supporting pupils with SEN. It is important that you recognise that the stresses experienced by such pupils and their families continue beyond school. Taking an interest in the lives of your pupils outside their classroom experiences will indicate to them that you care about their experiences and have an interest in them. Being well organised is an essential factor in enabling you to support learning outside school, whether this is preparing for a school trip or assisting a pupil with SEN to gain access to a local club or organisation.

Parents or carers will respect you not only for your ability as a class teacher, but also for your demonstration of care about the wider lives of their children. The pupils themselves will soon distinguish teachers who express a genuine interest in them and their activities from those who appear intent only on getting through the day's workload. The classroom is an important focus for much of the learning that you wish to impart to your pupils, but it is important to recognise that learning does not stop when the pupils go through the classroom door. Building upon the learning experiences of your pupils means taking an active interest in their out-of-school lives and recognising the opportunities to reinforce learning through use of resources outside the classroom.

Developing further as a professional

Overview

This chapter will address the following issues:

- identifying personal professional development needs
- becoming more reflective as a teacher
- using classroom-based enquiry to improve practice
- making use of the experiences of colleagues.

Introduction

Education is perpetually subjected to changing demands by legislation, new discoveries in educational research, and the fluctuating expectations of society. This inevitably presents challenges to you, as a teacher, as you try to keep abreast of developments and maintain high professional teaching standards. The field of special and inclusive education has been the focus of considerable attention by researchers and policy makers over the last 30 years, and this has inevitably meant that teachers concerned to address the needs of all pupils in their class have had to adopt new ideas and review their own practice. Many teachers welcome the challenge of change and the necessity to learn new skills or understand the latest theories, as it keeps their own thinking fresh and offers them new teaching experiences. Others find that the consequence of change is a source of increased stress and experience difficulty in keeping abreast of the many new expectations which come their way.

Teachers who are concerned to provide the best education for their pupils in inclusive primary classrooms need to accept that a commitment to professional development is essential. As Tilstone (2003) suggests, the acquisition of skills, knowledge and understanding is essentially a continuous process, but one that needs to respond to the needs of both individual teachers and the schools in which they work. You will inevitably find that at times the professional development priorities identified by school management may not dovetail exactly with what you perceive to be your own development needs. Part of your professionalism will be demonstrated through your ability to recognise both the necessity of being part of a school team with a commitment to meeting institutional needs, and an acceptance of responsibility for your own management of your professional development needs. This is not to suggest that the school in which you work does not have a responsibility to support your development, but rather to assert that you must have a realistic perception of the need to balance personal with whole-school needs.

When asked about the conditions that need to be created to accommodate pupils with SEN in their classrooms, teachers invariably point to more professional development specifically related to teaching pupils of diverse abilities as a priority (Cook, 2001; Romi and Leyser 2006; Rose, 2001). Many express concern that they are expected to teach pupils who exhibit needs or require approaches with which they are not familiar and for which they have received little training. You should, of course, anticipate that throughout your career you will face new challenges presented by pupils who have needs or require approaches and strategies with which you are unfamiliar. The individuality of all pupils should ensure that, as a professional, you are continually striving to understand more about how children learn and how to develop your skills as a teacher. To some extent, this is what it means to be professional. Just as you expect doctors to be conversant with current developments in medicine, so do you have a professional responsibility to keep abreast of changes in education.

Evidence-based practice

Cordingley (2004) emphasises that theoretical approaches to teaching and learning will find currency in schools only if they are seen to provide advice that is perceived by teachers as being feasible. Education has often been subjected to the vagaries of new initiatives and trends that seem to raise interest and generate enthusiasm for a period of time and then fade into the distance. New schemes for teaching maths or writing, for the management of behaviour or for the promotion of pupil relationships appear on the market and in our classrooms all of the time. Some of these are adopted by schools and become part of the regular armoury of approaches at the disposal of teachers; others, after a period of popularity, become redundant and disappear. Teachers are, quite rightly, always seeking ideas, resources and approaches to enhance their classroom performance and benefit their pupils. The truth is that there is no universal panacea for the challenges of learning. Pupils are individual in their needs, and teachers quickly develop a preferred method of working. When new initiatives are introduced into schools, some teachers will embrace them with enthusiasm, whilst others will be less sure and possibly even sceptical of their value. This is probably truer of systems introduced to support the learning of pupils with SEN than for most pupils.

Most new teachers entering the profession have had a fairly rudimentary introduction to the teaching of pupils with SEN during their initial teacher education (Garner, 1996; 2001). It is only when you enter the classroom and begin teaching on a regular basis that you will be able to identify which aspects of teaching pupils with SEN prove most challenging to you. As you begin your teaching career, you will find many experienced teachers and other colleagues willing to offer advice. This can be helpful, and it is certain that the finest resource in any school is its teachers, who usually bring a wealth of experience and expertise to the teaching situation. However, it is important to remember that even the most experienced teacher is unlikely to be able to offer an 'off-the-shelf' answer to all of the teaching challenges that you meet. Developing your teaching style and an understanding of how to encourage pupils to respond to your approach is personal to you and will take time to develop. You need to take advice and act upon it, but also to be aware of the need to adapt the ideas provided by others to your own situation. Furthermore, it is essential that you continually review your teaching to seek evidence of its impact upon the learning of the pupils in your charge.

Good teaching benefits all pupils regardless of need or ability. Developing teaching skills demands an appreciation that one approach, which may well be that which you prefer as a teacher, may elicit a positive response in the majority of pupils, but may not be so readily accessed by others. Teaching for the majority used to be the norm in many primary classrooms, but it is now generally accepted that an inclusive classroom is one in which the teacher recognises and addresses the needs of all learners. Good teachers are perpetually reviewing their work and gauging how pupils respond to their approaches. On the basis of this review, it is possible, with time and commitment, to identify those pupils who may require a different approach, such as some of those described in this book, and to make adjustments which ensure their participation. This requires the gathering of evidence related to your intended lesson outcomes and the responses of all the pupils in your class. Evidence of pupil response relates not only to academic performance and outcomes, though this is, of course, important, but also to pupil confidence and the ways in which pupils respond to you as a teacher. Successful teaching is founded upon positive relationships, and you will need to know how pupils feel about you as a person and recognise the ways in which your behaviour influences their learning.

Evidence-based teaching requires that you perpetually ask critical questions on your own performance, that of your pupils, and the resources and approaches used to provide access to learning. Garner and Davies (2001) provide a useful list of questions which teachers need to ask in order to keep abreast of their own teaching performance. These questions can provide a helpful starting point for review, particularly if they are incorporated into a system which enables you to collate evidence about your own teaching.

Key question[1]	Evidence
Do I encourage different types of learning? Which? How?	
What do I do to support these?	
Do I vary my teaching styles? Which? How?	
Do I promote flexible, collaborative learning?	
Do I plan my classroom with me or the children in mind?	
Are my structures clear and unambiguous?	
Do I teach all children?	
Do I give appropriate praise to all children?	
Do all children contribute?	
Do I provide alternative means of assessment/ success? Which?	

[1]Adapted from Garner and Davies (2001, p29).

The questions asked by Garner and Davies (2001) not only focus upon you as a teacher, but also emphasise the importance of establishing a good learning environment, recognising pupil individuality, assessing learning outcomes and building relationships. Each of these critical issues has been discussed in this book.

It is by asking such questions that you identify the ways in which you may acquire evidence about your own performance as a teacher. Changing your approach to suit a full range of pupils in your class will not be easy, but it will be more difficult if you do not have a commitment to personal professional development, and lack the evidence on which to base your future development as a teacher. Collecting evidence through observing and monitoring your own teaching and gaining insights into what works for both you and your pupils should become a key feature of your teaching. Wragg (1999) suggests that good teachers regularly observe their own teaching and, whenever the opportunity arises, that of their colleagues. He proposes self-evaluation as an important element of becoming a more effective classroom practitioner, but he also recognises that this is best achieved through the development of formal procedures based upon clear criteria and outcomes. This belief is further endorsed by Tilstone (1998), who recommends that the systematic collation of information through self-analysis may enable teachers to gain greater insights into their own teaching strengths and needs. Being systematic and having a definite focus are key elements of this process, as illustrated by the following case study.

Clare is a newly qualified teacher (NQT) working in a village primary school with a mixed Years 3 and 4 class. She enjoys teaching most sessions but is not very confident in physical education (PE) lessons and feels that she wants to improve her performance. She is particularly concerned that the most confident pupils in the class appear to engage well with physical activities but that a few are reluctant participants and lack the confidence to participate fully and enjoy lessons. She has kept records of her lessons over the last term, which indicate that two pupils, Alison, who is shy and quite timid about physical activity, and Jason, who has Down's syndrome and coordination problems, tend to remain on the periphery of activities.

At the beginning of this term, Clare observed the deputy head teacher, Margaret, teaching a movement lesson to a class of Year 6 pupils. She noticed that during the lesson pupils were encouraged to work in pairs and that Margaret was careful to partner pupils to ensure that the least confident pupils worked alongside others who were both competent and empathetic toward their classmates. After this observation of a more experienced teacher, Clare planned a series of movement lessons with Margaret and has introduced them to her class. She has evaluated her own performance by asking herself a series of critical questions closely related to some of those recommended by Garner and Davies (2001). This is a copy of her observations of her own performance.

Key questions	Evidence
Do I teach all children? Do they participate?	When pupils are working individually, Jason and Alison were still reluctant to join in. When I paired Jason with Thomas and Alison with Jade, they appeared to enjoy these partnerships. Whilst they still found the task difficult, they appeared more willing to have a go.
Do I give appropriate praise to all children?	I was particularly careful when asking the pupils to demonstrate what they had done in their pairs, to ensure that Jason and Thomas and Alison and Jade had an opportunity to show what they could do together. The whole class praised them for their work, and I think this made them feel better about the lesson.
Do the pupils enjoy the lesson?	Most of the pupils enjoy PE lessons. When I asked Jason and Alison about today's lesson, they said it was OK. Alison said it was better than last term's PE lessons.
Do I enjoy the lesson?	I am still not very confident in teaching these lessons, but I feel happier that I am now involving all of the pupils more than last term.
Do all children contribute?	The children were very willing to help each other, and for the first time I felt that for most of the lesson everyone joined in.

Clare's record shows that she has not only sought professional advice from a more experienced teacher, but has also been provided with specific professional development by observing Margaret teach. She has also taken away from her observation a number of teaching points, which she has planned into her own work with the support of Margaret. Her professional approach is further emphasised in her honest appraisal of her own performance. Here, Clare accepts that she is still not as confident as she would wish to be, but recognises some improvement in her performance and increasing confidence on the part of two pupils for whom she had concern.

On the basis of this experience, Clare decides to persist with this approach to teaching in her PE lessons and to discuss how she feels about each lesson with her class. She also asks Margaret to observe her teaching a PE lesson and to provide feedback and further advice.

This case study provides an example of a teacher taking responsibility for important elements of her own professional development. She has followed a sequence of events that can serve as a useful guide for all teachers who wish to improve their performance. This sequence can be described as:

- Reflect upon personal performance.
- Identify areas for development.
- Seek advice.
- Receive training.
- Act upon what has been learned.
- Evaluate the actions taken.
- Modify further actions on the basis of what has been learned.

Whilst, in the case study, Clare took a formal approach to this sequence, many teachers find it useful to go through the sequence regularly in order to ensure that they continue to improve as professionals.

Key questions and issues for reflection

- Are there some aspects of my teaching in which I am less confident than in others?
- Who in the school might be able to provide me with support and advice in improving my performance?
- What do the pupils think about the way in which I teach?
- Do all of the pupils participate at an appropriate level in my teaching?
- What further training opportunities do I feel I need?
- What further training opportunities are available to me?

Engaging with the development of teaching ideas

Teachers are among the most innovative and inventive members of our society. Visit any school and you are likely to find professional colleagues who have adapted teaching materials and approaches, devised new games or procedures, and identified ways of addressing problems that appear in their classrooms. New ideas about teaching and learning are generated by teachers and often remain within their classrooms. Whilst there are plentiful opportunities to disseminate new ideas through journals, professional magazines or teachers' conferences, many are destined to be lost or to reach only a limited audience within specific schools. However, the availability of numerous educational journals and books does to some extent compensate for this problem, and new teachers are well advised to ensure that they make use of these vital sources of information on a regular basis. Journals in particular provide information upon current educational innovations, often verified through research and establishing helpful links between theory and practice. Teachers who are determined to maintain their professional skills and standards find educational journals to be a source of valuable information and a means of keeping up to date with the latest ideas and practices to assist in addressing SEN. Journals such as the *British Journal of Special Education and Support for Learning* are full of useful ideas and discussion of research and practice focused upon young people who have difficulty in learning. Organisations such as nasen and the Social, Emotional and Behavioural Difficulties Association (SEBDA) run courses and conferences and provide a network of colleagues who are prepared to share their interest and expertise in teaching pupils with a wide range of needs and abilities. As a new teacher, you will find it invaluable to engage with such organisations and to gain access to the expert advice which they provide.

Attending specialist courses related to SEN and inclusion can assist in the development of new skills, knowledge and understanding. Many local authorities and universities run courses of varying length, some leading to accreditation and postgraduate qualifications. Early in your career, you may feel that taking on the extra work involved in an accredited course is more than you wish to tackle. New teachers often find it helpful to attend shorter local courses, specifically aimed at introducing approaches that are in common use but with which they may not be familiar. Many schools have a professional development coordinator who can provide details of professional development opportunities. It is worth remembering that, whilst providers of professional development can give you information, demonstrate techniques and suggest teaching approaches that are seen as beneficial for pupils with SEN, this will be of value only if you take the time to interpret the course content in relation to your own teaching situation. There are likely to be times when you attend a course and afterward cannot see its immediate benefits to your own situation. Having learned new skills, or knowledge on a course, experienced teachers often find that they can apply these several years later when a specific situation arises that demands the information gained. However, as a new teacher, when you undertake professional development, it is often helpful to prepare before the course by asking specific questions such as:

- What information, skills or understanding do I wish to learn?
- What skills, knowledge and understanding do I already have which I can build upon?
- Are there key questions that I want to ask the course provider?
- How do I hope this course might develop my professional skills?

After attending the course, it is helpful to discuss what you have learned with experienced colleagues in school. Some of your fellow teachers may well have experience of applying the ideas that you have picked up on the course. They may be able to contextualise your learning to the school situation or may be willing to help you reflect on the course content in respect of your classroom practice. After any course you attend it is worth completing a personal evaluation based upon a further set of questions:

- What were the key points that I picked up on the course?
- How do these points apply to my specific teaching situation?
- Do I wish to make changes to my practice based upon what I have learned?
- What are the implications of such changes?
- Do I have the necessary resources to implement these changes?
- How will I know if the changes are beneficial to my pupils?

If you do intend to make changes to your classroom environment or your practice after attending a course, be sure to discuss this with your immediate colleagues and the pupils. If you work regularly with a TA, ensure that you discuss the changes with that TA and discuss the reasons why you are making changes and how you hope this will benefit your teaching. Similarly, take time to discuss any changes with the pupils. They will learn more easily if they feel secure and confident in what you are doing. Introducing change can be unsettling for some pupils and will need to be managed carefully through discussion with them.

You should regard the self-evaluation of your teaching as a critical part of your professional practice. Asking questions about your own effectiveness, the impact of teaching approaches or resources, and the responses of pupils, including those with SEN should be given high priority. Good teachers are constantly reflecting upon their own practice and are committed to making adjustments wherever this is likely to lead to improvement and benefit for pupils.

One of the most effective ways to become more informed about the practice of teaching is to become actively engaged in classroom-based research. Personal enquiry in teaching can be a productive means of understanding what works best for you in a range of teaching and learning situations. Formalising your approach by asking critical questions about your classroom practice can be highly rewarding and can often provide insights into the ways that pupils learn and how you can best address their needs. The education of pupils with SEN has benefited greatly from classroom-based enquiry, and much of this has been based upon small-scale research undertaken by classroom teachers. Such a process may be conducted by individuals, by staff teams, or in partnership with colleagues from outside the school. Research is a process of asking critical questions and endeavouring to answer them through the implementation of structured enquiry. For many professions such as medicine or engineering, the use of structured research has become an accepted part of day-to-day practice. In teaching, we are only just beginning to appreciate the considerable value of systematic classroom investigation.

The value of educational research has been an issue of considerable debate over many years (Barrow and Foreman-Peck, 2005; Gomm and Hammersley, 2002), and it is clear that many teachers regard research as something done by academics with little relevance to teachers themselves. However, the influence of research upon practice should not be overlooked, and its value will become most evident to teachers who become actively involved in school-based enquiry. In the future, teachers need to exert more control over the research agenda, which has previously been set by policy makers and academics. The current generation of teachers, including you, as a new teacher, are much more likely to see educational research as a normal part of future school practice. Watkins (2006) suggests that teachers are most likely to be motivated to engage with educational research when they see that it has benefit for their own practice. She emphasises that the nature of research is not necessarily a large-scale investigation, but often begins with the identification of a teaching problem that a determined teacher chooses to examine through structured enquiry. Practitioner research of this nature has traditionally been pursued only as part of accredited, university-based courses, but is now being seen as a normal part of the development process by many schools. The use of action research has become increasingly popular in recent years as a means of enabling schools to solve problems related to SEN through investigation of specific areas of practice (Armstrong and Moore, 2004; Porter and Lacey, 2005). Such research need not require elaborate procedures but is best conducted within a structure that enables you, as the teacher, to ask critical questions of your own practice. The following case study demonstrates how two teachers in a primary school used a small-scale action research project to address a challenge within their school.

Sean teaches a class of mixed Years 3 and 4 pupils in a large, urban primary school. He has become concerned recently that one of his pupils with learning difficulties appears to have become somewhat distant from his peers during group activities. He knows that this pupil, Daniel, has been struggling with his work in most subjects and is concerned that because Daniel is so far behind, he is finding increasing difficulty in participating in group activities in which his classmates have made significantly more progress.

> After discussion with some of his teaching colleagues, Sean decides to investigate ways of making learning easier for Daniel. He plans a series of group activities in which Daniel will be required to take a leading role. He plans these activities for art lessons, a subject which Daniel enjoys and in which his learning difficulties do not appear so pronounced. Before the lesson, he goes through with Daniel a group activity that he wants completed during the session. He checks that Daniel is confident about what is required and helps him to practise some of the skills that will be required. At the start of the lesson, Sean tells Daniel and a small group with whom he will work during the lesson that he wants Daniel to organise and lead the group. Daniel has knowledge about the activity, gained from Sean's earlier instruction that the remainder of the group do not have.
>
> As the group work progresses, Sean is careful to observe how Daniel manages the situation and the reactions of his peers. After three art lessons using this approach, it has become clear that Daniel has gained in confidence and that there is increased engagement between himself and the others in the group.
>
> Over the next half-term, Sean asks the TA who works in his class to observe other group work situations to see if the improvements seen in art are generalised in other activities.

The preceding case study provides an example of a small-scale investigation to test the hypothesis that, by giving a pupil increased responsibility and a set of instructions, backed by some additional pre-lesson support, it may be possible to improve participation in group work. This is not a sophisticated piece of research, but does demonstrate how by being systematic in addressing a problem a teacher can conduct a small-scale enquiry to increase classroom practice.

On completion of his enquiry, Sean may wish to ask himself the following questions to assist in his continuing professional development:

- How can I build further upon this type of approach to encourage Daniel to develop further?
- Are there other pupils whom this approach might benefit?
- Is the additional time spent preparing a pupil in this way justified by the outcome?

It may be that Sean does not use this approach again for several years. However, it is quite possible that this use of personal enquiry may benefit many other pupils in the future.

Key questions and issues for reflection

- How clear am I about my own professional development needs?
- To what extent can I take greater control of my own professional development through reflection about my practice?
- How can I develop an enquiry-based approach to my professional learning?
- Who can advise/support me in adopting an enquiry-based approach?

Conclusion

Whilst schools have some responsibility for ensuring your continuing professional development, it is essential that you maintain a focus upon your developmental needs and endeavour to work toward ever-increasing professional standards. This will be achieved only through regular reflection and self-review, and by identifying opportunities to learn new skills, knowledge and understanding. There are more opportunities now for continuing professional development than ever before. You can take steps to secure your future career development and skills enhancement by discussing your professional development needs with relevant colleagues in school and identifying providers of effective training, and by formulating a personal professional development plan. Try making contact with your local university department of education and identify key providers within your local authority. They will undoubtedly be pleased to talk to you about current opportunities and should be able to assist you in designing a professional development programme to suit your own needs.

Teachers who are concerned to support pupils with SEN find that they get excellent support from professional organisations such as nasen, the National Autistic Society, and the Social, Emotional and Behavioural Difficulties Association. As a new teacher, you should consider joining an organisation of this type, where you will be able to make contact with other new teachers as well as highly experienced colleagues who will offer you support. In addition, such organisations provide access to excellent journals and often run their own professional development courses. In most areas of the UK, you will find local support groups focused upon a range of SEN such as dyslexia or behaviour difficulties. These afford similar opportunities to those provided by national organisations.

References

Abbott, C and Lucey, H (2005) Symbol communication in special schools in England: the current position and some key issues. *British Journal of Special Education*, 32: 196–201.

Ainscow, M (1995) Special needs through school improvement: school improvement through special needs, in Clark, C, Dyson, A and Millward, A (eds) *Towards inclusive schools?* London: David Fulton.

Ainscow, M (1999) *Understanding the development of inclusive schools.* London: Falmer.

Armstrong, D (2003) *Experiences of special education.* London: RoutledgeFalmer.

Armstrong, F and Moore, M (2004) *Action research for inclusive education.* London: Routledge.

Aronson, E, Blaney, N, Stephan, C, Sikes, J and Snapp, M (1978) *The Jigsaw Classroom.* Beverley Hills, CA: Sage.

Bailey, J (1998) Australia: inclusion through categorisation?, in Ainscow, M and Booth, T. (eds) *From them to us.* London: Routledge.

Barnes, R (1999) *Positive teaching, positive learning.* London: Routledge.

Barrow, R and Foreman-Peck, L (2005) *What use is educational research?* Impact 12. London: Philosophy of Education Society of Great Britain.

Bartholomew, L and Bruce, T (1993) *Getting to know you.* London: Hodder & Stoughton.

Barton, L (2003) The politics of education for all, in Nind, M, Rix, J, Sheehy, K and Simmons, K. (eds) *Inclusive education: diverse perspectives.* London: David Fulton.

Bastiani, J (1989) *Working with parents: a whole school approach.* Windsor: NFER-Nelson.

Bishop, A and Jones, P (2005) 'I never thought they would enjoy the fun of science just like ordinary children do' – exploring science experiences with early years teacher training students and children with severe and profound learning difficulties. *British Journal of Special Education:*, 303–43.

Blaney, N, Stephan, C, Rosenfield, D, Aronson, E and Sikes, J (1977) Interdependence in the classroom: a field study. *Journal of Educational Psychology*, 69: 121–8.

Boehm, A and Weinberg, R (1997) *The classroom observer* (3rd edn). New York: Teachers College Press.

Bondy, A and Frost, L (1994) The picture exchange communication system. *Focus on Autistic Behaviour*, 9: 1–19.

Booth, T, Ainscow, M and Dyson, A (1997) Understanding inclusion and exclusion in the English competitive education system. *International Journal of Inclusive Education*, 1: 337–55.

Bradley, C and Roaf, C (2000) Working effectively with learning support assistants, in Benton, P and O'Brien, T (eds) *Special needs and the beginnnig teacher*. London: Continuum.

Brower, F and Barber, M (2005) When words are not enough. *Special!* Autumn: 10–12

Byers, R (2001) Classroom processes, in Carpenter, B, Ashdown, R and Bovair, K (eds) *Enabling access: effective teaching and learning for pupils with learning difficulties* (2nd edn), Ch. 15. London: David Fulton.

Carpenter, B (2001) Enabling partnership: families and schools, in Carpenter, B, Ashdown, R and Bovair K (eds) *Enabling access: effective teaching and learning for pupils with learning difficulties* (2nd edn). London: David Fulton

Carpenter, B (2005) Early childhood intervention: possibilities and prospects for professionals, families and children. *British Journal of Special Education*, 32: 176–83

Carpenter, B and Morris, D (2001) 'English', in Carpenter, B, Ashdown, R and Bovair, K (eds) *Enabling access: effective teaching and learning for pupils with learning difficulties* (2nd edn). London: David Fulton.

Centre for Educational Needs, University of Manchester (1999) *The management, role and training of learning support assistants*. London: DfEE

Cockerill, S (2005) Are you sitting comfortably? *Special!* Autumn 19–23

Coffield, F, Mosley, D, Hall, E and Eccleston, K (2004) *Should we be using learning styles? What research has to say to practitioners*. [www.LSDA.org.uk].

Cook, B G (2001) A comparison of teachers' attitudes towards their included students with mild and severe disabilities. *Journal of Special Education* 34: 203–13.

Cordingley, P (2004) Teachers using evidence: using what we know about teaching and learning to reconceptualize evidence-based practice, in Thomas, G, and Pring R, (eds) *Evidence-based practice in education*. Buckingham: Open University Press.

Cremin, H, Thomas, G and Vincett, K (2003) Learning zones: an evaluation of three models for improving learning through teacher/teaching assistant teamwork. *Support for Learning*, 18: 154–61.

Cunningham, C and Davis, H (1985) *Working with parents: frameworks for collaboration*. Buckingham: Open University Press

Davis, P and Florian, L (2004) *Teaching strategies and approaches for pupils with special educational needs: a scoping study*. Nottingham: Department for Education and Skills Research Report 516.

DeClerq, H (2003) *Mum, is this an animal or a human being?* Bristol: Lucky Duck.

Department for Education and Employment (DfEE) (1996) *Education Act*. London: HMSO.

Department for Education and Employment (DfEE) (1997) *Excellence for all children*. London: The Stationery Office.

Department for Education and Employment (1998) *The National Literacy Strategy: framework for teaching*. London: DfEE.

Department for Education and Employment (DfEE) (2000) *The National Literacy Strategy: supporting pupils with special educational needs in the literacy hour*. London: DfEE.

Department for Education and Employment (DfEE)/Qualifications and Curriculum Authority (QCA) (1999) *The National Curriculum: Handbook for primary teachers in England*. London: DfEE/QCA.

Department for Education and Employment/Qualifications and Curriculum Authority (2000) *Curriculum Guidance for the Foundation Stage*. London: QCA.

Department of Education and Science (DES) (1978) *Report of the Committee of Enquiry into the Education of Handicapped Children and Young People* (The Warnock Report). London: HMSO.

Department for Education and Skills (DfES) (2001a) *Special Educational Needs Code of Practice*. London: DfES.

Department for Education and Skills (DfES) (2001b) *Inclusive schooling: children with special educational needs*. London: DfES.

Department for Education and Skills (DfES) (2002) *The National Literacy and Numeracy Strategies: Including all children in the literacy hour and daily mathematics lesson*. London: DfES.

Department for Education and Skills (DfES) (2003a) *The Report of the Special Schools Working Party*. Nottingham: DfES.

Department for Education and Skills (DfES) (2003b) *Excellence and enjoyment: a strategy for primary schools*. London: DfES.

Department for Education and Skills (DfES) (2004a) *The Children Act*. London: HMSO.

Department for Education and Skills (DfES) (2004) *Removing barriers to achievement, the government's strategy for SEN*. London: DfES.

Ellins, J and Porter, J (2005) Departmental differences in attitudes to special educational needs in the secondary school. *British Journal of Special Education*, 32: 188–95.

English, E and Newton, L (2005) *Professional studies in the primary school. Thinking beyond the standards*. London: David Fulton.

Every Child Matters (2003) London: The Stationery Office.

Exley, S (2005) The effectiveness of teaching strategies for students with dyslexia based on their preferred learning styles. *British Journal of Special Education*, 30: 213–20.

Farrell, M (2003) *Understanding special educational needs*. London: RoutledgeFalmer.

Farrell, P (1997) *Teaching pupils with learning difficulties: strategies and solutions*. London: Cassell.

Farrell, P (1999) Special education in the last twenty years: have things really got better? *British Journal of Special Education*, 28: 3–9.

Farrell, P and Balshaw, M (2002) Can teaching assistants make special education inclusive?, in Farrell, P and Ainscow, M (eds) *Making special education inclusive*. London: David Fulton.

Fletcher, W (2001) Enabling pupils with severe learning difficulties to become effective target setters, in Rose, R and Grosvenor, I (eds) *Doing research in special education*. London: David Fulton.

Florian, L (1998) Inclusive practice: what, why and how?, in Tilstone, C, Florian, L and Rose, R (eds) *Promoting inclusive practice*. London: Routledge.

Florian, L and Rouse, M (2001) Inclusive practice in English secondary schools: lessons learned. *Cambridge Journal of Education*, 31: 399–412.

Frith, U (1989) *Autism: explaining the enigma*. Oxford: Blackwell.

Gardner, H (1983) *Frames of mind: the theory of multiple intelligences*. New York: Basic Books.

Gardner, H (1993) *Multiple intelligences: the theory in practice*. New York: Basic Books.

Gardner, H (1999) *Intelligence reframed: multiple intelligence for the 21st century*. New York: Basic Books.

Garner, P (1996) A special education? The experience of newly qualified teachers during initial training. *British Educational Research Journal*, 22: 155–63.

Garner, P (2001) Goodbye, Mr Chips: special needs, inclusive education and the deceit of initial teacher training, in O'Brien T (ed.), *Enabling inclusion: blue skies...dark clouds*. London: The Stationery Office.

Garner, P and Davies, JD (2001) *Introducing special educational needs*. London: David Fulton.

Giangreco, MF (1997) Key lessons learned about inclusive education: summary of the 1996 Schonell memorial lecture. *International Journal of Disability*. 44: 193–206.

Gomm, R and Hammersley, M (2002) Research and practice: two worlds forever at odds?, in Hammersley, M (ed.) *Educational research: policy making and practice*. London: Paul Chapman Publishing.

Grandin, T (1995) *Thinking in pictures and other reports from my life with autism*. New York: Doubleday.

Gray, C (1998) Social stories and comic strip conversations with students with Asperger syndrome and high functioning autism, in Schopler, E, Mesibov, G and Kunce, L (eds), *Asperger syndrome or high functioning autism?* (pp 167–98). New York: Plenum Press.

Griffiths, M and Davis, C (1995) *In fairness to children*. London: David Fulton.

Gross, J (1996) *Special educational needs in the primary school*. Buckingham: Open University Press.

Hayes, J (2004) Visual annual reviews: how to include pupils with learning difficulties in their educational reviews. *Support for Learning*, 19: 175–80.

Helavaara Robertson, L and Hill, R (2001) Excluded voices: educational exclusion and inclusion, in Hill, D and Cole M (eds) *Schooling and Equality*. London: Kogan Page.

Howley, M (2006) Structured teaching for pupils with autistic spectrum disorders: meaningful or meaningless? *REACH Journal of Special Needs Education in Ireland,* 19: 94–101.

Howley, M and Arnold, E (2005) *Revealing the hidden social code: social stories™ for people with autistic spectrum disorders*. London: Jessica Kingsley.

Howley, M and Kime, S (2003) Policies and practice for the management of individual learning needs, in Rose, R and Tilstone, C *Strategies to promote inclusive practice*. London: Routledge.

Howley, M and Preece, D (2003) Structured teaching for individuals with visual impairments. *British Journal of Visual Impairment* 21: 78–83.

Howley, M, Preece, D and Arnold, T (2001) Multi-disciplinary use of 'structured teaching' to promote consistency of approach for children with autistic spectrum disorder. *Education and Child Psychology* 18: 41–52.

Howley, M and Rose, R (2003) Facilitating group work for pupils with autistic spectrum disorders by combining jigsawing and structured teaching. *Good Autism Practice (GAP),* 4 : 20–5.

Hume, T (2005) Different needs and different responses, in English, E and Newton, L (eds) *Professional studies in the primary school. Thinking beyond the standards* pp 124–39 London: David Fulton.

Jenkins, JR and O'Connor, RE (2003) Co-operative learning for students with learning disabilities: evidence from experiments, observations and interviews, in Graham, S, Harris K and Swanson, L (eds) *Handbook of learning disabilities*. New York: Guilford.

Johnson, DW, Johnson, RT, and Johnson-Holubec, EJ (1990) *Circles of learning*. Edina, MN: Interactive Book Company.

Jordan, R and Powell, S (1990) Autism and the national curriculum. *British Journal of Special Education* 17: 140–42.

Joyce, B, Calhoun, E and Hopkins, D (2002) *Models of learning, tools for teaching.* Buckingham: Open University Press.

Jupp, K (1992) *Everyone belongs: mainstream education for children with severe learning difficulties.* London: Souvenir Press.

Kershner, R (2000) Teaching children whose progress in learning is causing concern, in Whitebread, D, (ed.) *The psychology of teaching and learning in the primary school.* London: RoutledgeFalmer.

Kershner, R and Florian, L (2004) *Teaching strategies for pupils with 'special educational needs': specialist or inclusive pedagogy?* Paper presented to the European Conference on Educational Research, Crete.

Kornhaber, M, Fierros, E and Veenema, S (2004) *Multiple intelligences: best ideas from research and practice.* Boston: Pearson, Allyn and Bacon.

Kunce, L and Mesibov, B (1998) Educational approaches to high-functioning autism and Asperger syndrome, in Schopler, E Mesibov G B and Kunce, L (eds) *Asperger syndrome or high functioning autism?* New York: Plenum Press.

Lacey, P (2001) *Support partnerships: collaboration in action.* London: David Fulton.

Latham, C and Miles, A (2001) *Communication, curriculum and classroom practice.* London: David Fulton.

Leggett, T (2005) Behaviour management. in English, E and Newton, L (eds) *Professional studies in the primary school. Thinking beyond the standards,* London: David Fulton.

Lewis, A (1992) From planning to practice. *British Journal of Special Education* 19: 24–7.

Lewis, A (2000) *Mapping pedagogy for special educational needs.* Paper presented at ISEC, the International Special Education Congress, University of Manchester, 24–28 July.

Lewis, A and Norwich, B (2001) A critical review of systematic evidence concerning distinctive pedagogies for pupils with difficulties in learning. *Journal of Research in Special Educational Needs.* 1: 2–9.

Lumsden, E (2005) Joined up thinking in practice: an exploration of professional collaboration in Waller, T (ed.) *An introduction to early childhood.* London: Paul Chapman Publishing.

Marvin, C (1998) Individual and whole class teaching, in Tilstone, C, Florian, L, and Rose, R, (eds) *Promoting inclusive practice.* London: Routledge.

McLeod, F (2001) Towards inclusion – our shared responsibility for disaffected pupils. *British Journal of Special Education.* 28: 191–94.

Mercer, CD and Mercer, AR (1998) *Teaching students with learning problems* (5th edn). Upper Saddle River, NJ: Prentice-Hall.

Mesibov, G and Howley, M (2003) *Accessing the curriculum for pupils with autistic spectrum disorders.* London: David Fulton.

Mittler, P (2000) *Working towards inclusive education.* London: David Fulton.

Mortimer, H (2001) *Special needs and early years provision.* London: Continuum.

Murphy, E, Grey, IM and Honan, R (2005) Co-operative learning for students with difficulties in learning: a description of models and guidelines for implementation. *British Journal of Special Education* 32: 157–64.

Newton, C, Wilson, D and Taylor, G (1996) Circles of friends: an inclusive approach to meeting emotional and behavioural needs. *Educational Psychology in Practice,* 11: 41–8.

Newton, D (2005) Teaching and learning in the primary school, in English, E and Newton, L (eds) *Professional studies in the primary school. Thinking beyond the standards.* London: David Fulton.

Newton, L (2005) The reflective practitioner, in English, E and Newton, L (eds) *Professional studies in the primary school. Thinking Beyond the Standards*. London: David Fulton.

Noble, K (2003) Personal reflection on experiences of special and mainstream education in Shevlin, M, and Rose, R (eds) *Encouraging voices*. Dublin: National Disability Authority.

Norwich, B (1996) Special needs education or education for all? Connective specialisation and ideological impurity. *British Journal of Special Education,* 23: 100–04.

Nutbrown, C (1996) Questions for respectful educators, in Nutbrown, C (ed.) *Children's rights and early education*. London: Paul Chapman Publishing.

O'Brien, T and Guiney, D (2001) *Differentiation in teaching and learning*. London: Continuum.

Office for Standards in Education (OfSTED) (2004) *Special educational needs and disability*. London: OfSTED.

O'Riordan, M and Plaisted, KC (2001) Enhanced discrimination in autism. *Quarterly Journal of Experimental Psychology*, 54: 961–79.

O'Riordan, M, Plaisted, KC, Driver, J and Baron-Cohen, S (2001) Superior visual search in autism. *Journal of Experimental Psychology: Human Perception and Performance,*: 719–30.

Ott, P (1997) *How to detect and manage dyslexia: A reference and resource manual*. Oxford: Heinemann.

Ozonoff, S (1995) Executive functions in Autism, in Schopler, E and Mesibov, GB (eds) *Learning and cognition in autism*. New York: Plenum Press.

Peeters, T (1997) *Autism: from theoretical understanding to educational intervention*. London: Whurr.

Polat, F, Kalambouka, A and Boyle, W (2002) Building tomorrow together: effective transition planning for pupils with special educational needs, in Farrell, P and Ainscow, M (eds) *Making special education inclusive*. London: David Fulton

Porter, J and Lacey, P (2005) *Researching learning difficulties*. London: Paul Chapman Publishing.

Powell, S (2000) *Helping children with autism to learn*. London: David Fulton.

Read, G (1998) Promoting inclusion through learning styles, in Tilstone, C, Florian, L and Rose, R (eds) *Promoting inclusive practice*. London: Routledge.

Riding, RJ and Cheema, I (1991) Cognitive styles: an overview and integration. *Educational Psychology*, 11: 193–215.

Romi, S and Leyser, Y (2006) Exploring inclusion pre-service training needs: a study of variables associated with attitudes and self-efficacy beliefs. *European Journal of Special Needs Education*. 21: 85–105.

Rose, R (1991) A jigsaw approach to group work. *British Journal of Special Education*. 18: 54–8.

Rose, R (2000) Using classroom support in a primary school: a single case study. *British Journal of Special Education,* 27: 191–96.

Rose, R (2001) Primary school teacher perceptions of the conditions required to include pupils with special educational needs. *Educational Review,* 53: 147–56.

Rose, R and Coles, C (2002) Special and mainstream school collaboration for the promotion of inclusion. *Journal of Research in Special Educational Needs*, 2 (2): 51–72.

Sainsbury, C (2000) *Martian in the playground*. Bristol: Lucky Duck.

Sanders, D, White, G, Burge, B, Sharp, C, Eames, A, McEune, R and Grayson, H (2005) *A study of the transition from the Foundation Stage to Key Stage 1*. DfES Research Report SSU/2005/FR/013). London: Department for Education and Skills.

Sanger, J (1996) *The complete observer? A field research guide to observation.* London: Falmer Press.

Schopler, E, Mesibov, GB and Hearsey, K (1995) Structured teaching in the TEACCH system, in Schopler, E and Mesibov, GB (eds.) *Learning and cognition in autism.* New York: Plenum Press.

Shaw, S and Hawes, T (1998) *Effective teaching and learning in the primary classroom: a practical guide to brain compatible learning.* Optimal Learning.

Smith, A (1996) *Accelerated learning in the classroom.* Stafford: Network Educational Press.

Souza, A (1995) My experiences of schooling, in Potts., P, Armstrong, F, and Masterton, M (eds) *Equality and diversity in education: learning, teaching and managing in schools.* London: Routledge.

Tilstone, C (1998) *Observing teaching and learning.* London: David Fulton.

Tilstone, C (2003) Professional development of staff, in Tilstone, C, and Rose R, (Eds.) *Strategies to promote inclusive practice.* London: Routledge.

Todd Broun, L (2004) Teaching students with autistic spectrum disorders to read: A visual approach. *Journal of the Council for Exceptional Children,* 36: 36–40.

Toolan, D (2003) Shaped identities, in Shevlin, M, and Rose, R (eds) *Encouraging voices.* Dublin: National Disability Authority.

Vygotsky, LS (1982) *On the child's psychic development.* Copenhagen: Nyt Nordisk.

Waine, L and Kime, S (2005) Practical Aspects of Assessment, in Backhouse, G and Morris, K (eds) *Dyslexia? assessing and reporting: The Patoss guide,* Ch 3. London: Hodder Murray.

Watkins, A (2006) So what exactly do teacher-researchers think about doing educational research? *Support for Learning,* 21: 12–18.

Whitaker, P (2004) Fostering communication and shared play between mainstream peers and children with autism: approaches, outcomes and experiences. *British Journal of Special Education,* 31: 215–22.

Whitaker, P, Barrat, P, Joy, H, Potter, M and Thomas, G (1998) Children with autism and peer group support: using 'circles of friends'. *British Journal of Special Education,* 25:60–4.

Wilkins, T and Nietfield, JL (2004) The effect of a school-wide inclusion training programme upon teachers attitudes about inclusion. *Journal of Research in Special Educational Needs.* 4: 115–21.

Wing, L and Gould, J (1979). Severe impairments of social interaction and associated abnormalities in children: epidemiology and classification. *Journal of Autism and Childhood Schizophrenia,* 9: 11–29.

Wragg, EC (1999) *An introduction to classroom observation* (2nd ed). London: Routledge.

Wright, J, Newton, C, Clarke, M, Donlan, C, Lister, C and Cherguit, J (2006) Communication aids in the classroom: the views of education staff and speech and language therapists involved with the Communication Aids Project. *British Journal of Special Education* 33: 25–32.

Author Index

Subject Index